PREAMBLE

Hello and thank you for purchasing this book, which I hope will become your best tool for your RV or your future RV.

Why read this book? Because if you are like me, you would rather enjoy your vacation than waste your time troubleshooting your RV. You'll save time and money instead of thinking, I should have checked this, serviced that while you're stranded on the side of the road. Instead, you'll spend that precious time lying on your lounge chair sipping your favorite cocktail at the place you planned to go.

In addition, I plan to improve this book over time by following trends and adding sections to better answer your questions. By the way, you can write to me at: **travelerguiderv@gmail.com**

I am passionate about RVing. RVing has been a part of my life since I was very young, starting with my parents, and has never stopped. My experience comes from this passion combined with the many jobs I have done and continue to do. This forces me to always want to know more to find solutions to as many problems as possible. As a child, I always wanted to know how things worked, starting with my toys. I started by repairing my bikes, my motorcycles, my cars and then I became an electro-mechanic. Always thirsty for knowledge, I then became a building mechanic technician and today I lead a team of multidisciplinary workers in the field of maintenance, I am an entrepreneur and now I can add this book to my list of experience.

I am fortunate to be able to leave in my RV several weeks a year and to travel all over the world. During my travels, I've encountered problems like everyone else, but nothing insurmountable. It's part of the adventure. By leafing through magazines, by browsing through RV enthusiast groups on Facebook, by traveling with other campers, in short, many sources inspired me to create this book. My first tip? The preparation and knowledge I will share with you in this book. I will share with you my experience and all the things I wish I had known when I started in the wonderful world of RVing.

First, I will help you choose your RV and tow vehicle. Once chosen, I will teach you the theoretical basics, of course, of driving with an RV. This will make it easier for you to practice. Then, how your RV works. In my opinion, this is the basis if you want to do a good maintenance without pulling your hair out. Then long-term maintenance and storage. After reading the chapters on operation and storage, you will have a much better understanding of how and why the various components are maintained.

Finally, the troubleshooting section. Despite the fact that you have done everything possible to save yourself and minimize the chances of it happening, a breakdown could still occur. What do I do if I have a breakdown? Assuming you know how it works from part #4 and how to maintain it, troubleshooting will be much easier. I will explain to you the things to check and how to troubleshoot in case of a breakdown.

HOW TO CHOOSE YOUR RV

How to choose your RV. The criteria, advantages and disadvantages of each type.

The purpose of this chapter is to help you choose your RV according to your needs. I do not express my opinion since it is your choice and only you know your needs. I will elaborate criteria, advantages and disadvantages in the most neutral way possible. I am in my forties, I have a wife and two young daughters and my criteria are probably very far from those of a single person or a retired couple for example. It is imperative to evaluate your needs when shopping for an RV. You will discover first the criteria for buying and then the advantages and disadvantages of each type later in the chapter.

I have owned a few RVs in my life and I also have the opportunity to store for them. I know how easy it can be to get lost with many different types of models and options. As for the criteria, only you can answer them. So here's a list of questions you should ask yourself when purchasing your RV:

- Will you use your RV year-round or only in the summer?

- Where will I store the RV when it is not in use in the summer or winter?

- How much space does my RV take up during storage time?

- Will you favor highways or back roads on your trips?

- How much sleeping space will you need?

- Do you have young children who will be with you for a long time or do you have teenagers?

- Will your passengers, people with disabilities or pets have special needs?

- Are you a wilderness camping type, full service or both?

- Do you want privacy with your passengers or is that not important?

- Do you need a lot of storage space?

- What is the towing capacity of your vehicle?

- What is your budget?

- New or used?

Let's elaborate on that last point a bit. **New or used?** Here, in my experience of having been around both sides, are the pros and cons of new and used.

Benefits Of New:

- Better warranty
- You will have a choice of what options you want to put on it.
- Should basically last longer.
- Financial loans can be spread out over a longer period of time.

Disadvantages Of New:

- Having too many choices often becomes easier to get lost in and make the wrong choices.

• You may be returning to the dealer for multiple adjustments and repairs more often than second hand. You'll understand this last point in the next few lines.

• Prices are higher.

Here is my experience with new. I bought a new trailer and I admit I spent much, much more time shopping for them but I found exactly what I wanted according to my criteria. So far, it's not too much of a problem if you like shopping. I was able to spread out my payments over a period equivalent to a home mortgage. It's nice, everything is new and it smells new. We were very excited about our purchase, wasted no time and rushed to make our first trip. To make a long story short, everything went well to get to our destination and on the ground proud of our new purchase. On the way back, we had about 200 kilometers to go. Suddenly, about a kilometer from our home, fortunately, the fresh water tank fell over while we were driving. It was about half full. A support under the trailer was not strong enough and boom! It broke. I was able to get home with a half-hung tank lying on the ground. Well, don't panic, it's guaranteed.

All this to say that even new, there can be problems. If, however, we had had a second hand one in this particular case, chances are that this test would have been done before us and the problem would have been solved. If you decide to buy an RV that has already been sold in thousands of units before you get yours, the chances of glitches like this are reduced. Many people before you have tested it, so in theory the manufacturer has corrected the problem. It's a bit like a car, the first year it's on the market, not all problems are solved. The cars on the other hand, are tested before being put on the market to make them as reliable as possible. The laws are particularly strict in this respect. There is more room for maneuver in the RV market unfortunately. So don't take for granted that because it's new, you won't have any problems. That's often our first instinct. I'm not saying that this kind of problem happens frequently either, but the risk decreases with use.

I now come to the second hand.

The Benefits Of Second Hand:

• Price at least 20% less than new depending on the age of the RV.

• Design issues have mostly been addressed.

Disadvantages Of Second Hand:

• Shorter warranty and nonexistent if you buy from a private party.

• You only have a choice of what's on the market.

• Loan is more complicated to get.

• Shortened life span depending on the age and quality of maintenance that was done before you.

Here is my experience with second hand. We had to drop a few criteria for our purchase but even so we were very happy with our purchase. We opted for a brand that has a proven track record for reliability and we were not disappointed. It's the Citation brand, I'll take the liberty of mentioning it since this brand has unfortunately not existed for several years. It was already 3 or 4 years old and we had paid 40 to 50% less than a similar new one. We bought it from a dealer. For my part, I strongly recommend it. You won't necessarily pay more and the dealer is obliged to offer you a warranty and sell you a fully functional RV. If it is not, he must inform you in writing. This does not mean that the brakes and tires will be new, as this is normal wear and tear and the dealer is not required to replace them if they are functional. As for private individuals, we can't hide it, sometimes they don't sell for nothing and won't necessarily tell you the real reason for the sale. You have to be more vigilant and do more verification. You could end up with problems and not realize it until you are thousands of miles away from the previous owner. If you follow the tips in this book, you'll be more alert and more able to know what to check. In the end, a second-hand RV could still last a very long time if you take good care of it.

Before you buy, also consider the following. When traveling, pulling or carrying a trailer affects fuel consumption depending on weight, wind resistance, properly inflated tires, tow vehicle capacity, etc. It's hard to accurately determine fuel consumption with so many factors. To maximize your fuel economy, make sure your tires, vehicle and RV, are inflated according to the manufacturer's recommendations on the tire. Also, from one tow vehicle to another with the same RV, there can be a good difference in fuel economy. In my experience, the closer you get to the tow vehicle's maximum towing capacity, the more fuel it will consume. A more powerful vehicle will run out of steam less and consume less.

Here is a formula to estimate the **fuel consumption** of your vehicle towing or transporting a trailer. This calculation is for information purposes only to make you aware of the cost of moving an RV.

According to a study (U.S. departement of energy), each 100kg(220lbs) is equivalent to about 0,5L/100km or each 100lbs(45kg) is equivalent to 1% less mpg(miles per gallon):

Consumption L/100KM for a weight of 2200kg(+/- 5000lbs) :

2200kg/100kg = 22

22 x 0.5L/100km = **11L/100km** to add for your caravan or total weight of your motorhome

Or in mpg

Consumption MPG for a weight of 5000lb(+/- 2200kg) :

5000lbs/100 = 50

50 x 1% = 50%

For a vehicle consuming 23mpg: 23mpg - 50% = **11.5mpg**

This is an estimate, many other factors come into play but it gives you a good starting point.

Add the weight of everything in the caravan for more precision. Fresh water, waste water, food, propane, bikes, etc...

Don't forget that you may need other things to fill your RV and enjoy it. **Here is a list of things to bring to your RV** that will affect your budget outside of the purchase of your RV. Will you need...

- A new bike rack?
- A towing kit?
- To register your RV?
- Purchase an electrical extension? 15 amp or 30 amp?
- Hose and adapters for sewage disposal?
- A drinking water supply hose?
- A BBQ if you don't already have one?
- An additional refrigerator?

• An additional generator? If you can't put it inside the RV then will you need a storage box and stand for it?

• Propane tanks?

• Stabilizer jacks to level your trailer?

• Things for your kitchen? Dishes, utensils, coffee maker, toaster, microphone oven, bowls, knives, can opener, airtight container, aluminum foil, etc...

• Bedding? Sheets, pillows, etc...

• Extra storage? Furniture, laundry rack, drying rack, shelves, etc...

Other criteria will undoubtedly be added depending on the type of RV you choose.

So, to help you in the next few pages, here are the types of RVs, their advantages and disadvantages.

The types are:

• Mounted trailers
• Micro trailers
• Tent trailers
• Hybrid trailers
• Trailers
• Fifth wheel trailers
• Motorized Class A
• Motorized Class B
• Motorized Class C

TRUCK CAMPERS

Truck campers are those that are loaded onto the chassis or bed of a pickup truck. Be sure to check because not just any pickup truck will accommodate a travel trailer. Ask your dealer for more information. Keep in mind the dimensions and weight of the unit. The location of wheel humps and the spacing between them, the height and distance from the bottom of the truck bed. The length of your van body and the location of the rear lights. It is essential that the dimensions of the trailer fit your van. You need to know the maximum capacity your van can carry before you buy. Also consider your own weight, the weight of the water in the tanks and all the things you will be putting in it.

Average length of 3.6 to 6 M (12 to 20 feet)

Dry weight from 450kg (1000 lbs) to over 1800kg (4000 lbs)

Maximum capacity of 4 people

New price range from $15000 to $55000

Benefits

● Economical option for anyone who already owns a pickup truck.

● Compact size for easy moving and parking.

● The rear remains free to tow a trailer with a boat, ATV, snow-mobile, etc...

● The unit can rest on its jacks leaving the vehicle free for other movements.

● Some models even have a toilet, shower, kitchen and/or air conditioning.

● Some models can be used in winter. Better insulation, heating.

● Easy storage

● More economical in gasoline

Disadvantages

● Less privacy due to limited space. Often only one room.

● Finding the right trailer that fits the right truck.

● Becomes complicated when it comes time to change vans to find one that fits our trailer.

● Depending on the weight and your truck, you may need to con-sider reinforcing the suspension with balloons.

● Limited storage space. In addition the caravan takes up the space of the box of the truck that could have served as storage.

MICRO CAMPERS

Micro campers are trailers that can be transported with a car or a small everyday SUV or even a three wheels motorcycle and an electric vehicle. With a maximum weight of 1150 kg (2500 lbs) If it is not recommended to tow anything with your vehicle, it is better not to tow anything with it. Many vehicles can pull up to 450kg (1000 lbs). These vehicles will do the job for most micro caravans as long as this weight is not exceeded. If you do decide to tow this type of trailer on a vehicle not designed for it, you will have to make sure that the engine and transmission do not over-heat or you could have problems with premature wear, transmission slippage or worse, engine or transmission failure. This not only makes vacations expensive but also shortens them.

Average length between 3M (10ft) and 4.5M (18ft)

Dry weight from 225kg (500lbs) to 1150kg (2500lbs)

Maximum capacity of 2 people

New price range from 7500$ to 20000$.

Benefits

● Very maneuverable, light weight and not much grip in the wind on the road.

● Can be pulled by virtually any vehicle.

● Some are even almost as equipped as a larger trailer. Toilet, shower, television, air conditioning, etc...

● Can be left on the campground only use the tow vehicle when visiting.

● We can leave our belongings inside, clothes, food, etc...

● Affordable

● Easy to store

● Can be installed on the majority of campgrounds

Disadvantages

● The more options we add, the heavier it easily becomes and exceeds the maximum weight of our towing vehicle. We have to limit ourselves in our possible options.

● The fuel consumption of the towing vehicle will increase all the same according to the weight.

● Limited privacy due to limited space. Often only one room.

● Limited storage space. Depending on the model, often you can't stand on it.

TENT TRAILERS

Tent trailers are a hybrid of tents and trailers. Reminiscent of the camping experience of a tent but with the amenities of a trailer. Taking the advantages and disadvantages of both. The folded dimensions are roughly equivalent to micro trailers but once the canvas ends are unfolded, the space is almost doubled and some models even more. Heavier than the micro-trailers but still of a reasonable weight to be pulled by an SUV, a minivan and sometimes by a mid-size car. In the same price range as the micro-trailers and some, even more affordable.

Average unfolded length between 4.6M (15ft) and 7M (23ft)

Average dry weight between 450kg (1000lbs) and 1350kg (3000lbs)

Maximum capacity up to 8 people

New price range from $10,000 to $25,000

Benefits

● Can be left in the field and used only as a tow vehicle to visit.

● Easy to maneuver.

● Lightweight.

● Can be installed on most campgrounds.

● Affordable.

● Low windage on the road.

● Can be left with food, clothing, etc... inside.

● Some have all the amenities like stove, toilet and shower.

Disadvantages

● Limited privacy.

● Weak soundproofing.

● Longer and sometimes tedious installation time.

● Unable to get inside when folded.

● Must be reassembled often once back home if folded soak and only even dampened. Otherwise, mold alert.

HYBRID TRAILERS

Hybrid trailers are a cross between a hard sided trailer and a tent trailer. They have one or more sliding sections at the ends to deploy sleeping berths. They are generally more adorable and lighter than a trailer. They can therefore be towed by a larger number of family vehicles.

Average length between 5.8M (19ft) and 8.2M (29ft)

Average dry weight between 1100kg (2500lbs) and 2200kg (5000lbs)

Capacity up to 8 people

Price range between 12000$ and 35000$.

Benefits

- Usually lighter than a trailer and can be towed by an SUV. Some lightweight versions can be towed by automobiles with 6-cylinder engines.

- Bunk beds that fold out add space and up to 8 people.

- Perfect for a young family.

- Includes all amenities.

Disadvantages

- Poor soundproofing, especially in the folding bunks.

- Must be reassembled often once back home if it has been folded soak and only even dampened. Otherwise, alert mildew.

- Still needs a vehicle powerful enough to be towed.

- A little more difficult to maneuver.

TRAILERS

Trailers are designed to be towed by a large SUV or pickup truck. The most popular type to live in for a longer period of time while offering the comfort of a home. A wide variety of models with extensions, garage, terrace, bay window, office, bunk beds, etc... There is certainly a model that suits you. Often used as a seasonal residence.

Average length between 5,8M (19ft) and 11M (36ft)

Average dry weight between 1800KG (4000lbs) and 4500KG (10000lbs)

Capacity up to 10 people

Price range between 19000$ and 120 000$.

Benefits

- Several varieties of models for all tastes.
- All the amenities of a fireplace.
- Despite the size length, does not require a special permit.
- More privacy.
- Sets up quickly on the campground.

Disadvantages

- Requires a large vehicle for towing.
- Difficult to back up and maneuver. Requires practice.
- More difficult to find a campsite if not reserved in advance.
- High weight causes the tow vehicle to use a lot of gas.

FIFTH WHEEL TRAILERS

The fifth wheel trailers are designed to be towed by a van equipped with a special hitch on the platform. Designed on two levels, they are very welcoming and have all the amenities of a home. Some models are really luxurious and very spacious with the possibility of a terrace, garage and up to 5 extensions.

Average length between 6.4M (21ft) and 12.2M (40ft)

Average dry weight between 2700KG (6000lbs) and 7250KG (16000lbs)

Capacity up to 8 people

Price range between $35000 and $170,000

Benefits

- All the amenities and more.
- Most comparable caravan to a house.
- More privacy the majority of the time at least one closed room.
- Despite the size length, does not require a special permit.
- Sets up quickly on the campground.

Disadvantages

- Absolutely requires an adapted and sufficiently powerful van.
- Takes up a lot of storage space in the van's box.
- Steps inside less convenient for people with limited mobility.
- Difficult to back up and maneuver. Requires practice.
- More difficult to find a campsite if not reserved in advance.
- High weight causes the tow vehicle to use a lot of gas.

CLASS A MOTORHOMES

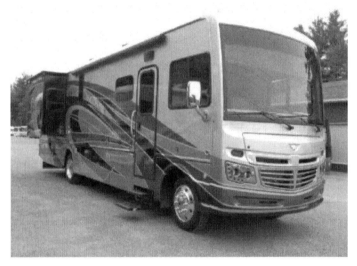

Class A motorhomes are the largest motorhomes. They are built on a bus base with a flat nose. This is the most luxurious category in my opinion, where the prices have almost no limit. They can have almost anything your imagination could think of. It's really a house with a motor. It usually has all the amenities of a home. You can attach a vehicle to the back of it often without any problem.

Average length between 8M (27ft) and 13.5M (45ft)

Capacity up to 12 people

Price range from $80,000 to over $1 million

Benefits

- All the amenities and more.

- A home with a motor.

- More privacy the majority of the time at least one closed room.

- Despite the great length, it does not require a special permit. Check anyway depending on the country from which you will travel.

- Sets up quickly on the campsite.

- Can pull larger vehicles.

- Often lots of trunk storage all around.

- Often huge gas tank to easily go over 1000 km without stopping at gas stations.

Disadvantages

- Difficult to maneuver. Requires practice.

- More difficulties to find a camping site if you don't reserve in advance.

- High weight results in high gasoline or diesel consumption.

CLASS B MOTORHOMES

Class B motorhomes are the smallest in the motorhome category although some can go up to 7.5M ft (25ft) or more. Usually built on a van base. From Westfalia to Mercedes vans. They can have a kitchen, bathroom and other amenities similar to a small house.

Average length between 4.5M (15ft) and 7.5M (25ft)

Sleeps up to 4 people

Price range between 45000$ and 125000$.

Benefits

- Easy to maneuver and park.
- Lightweight.
- Can fit in most campgrounds.
- Low wind load on the road.
- Can be left with food, clothing, etc... inside.
- Some have all the amenities like stove, toilet and shower.

Disadvantages

- Limited privacy.
- Poor soundproofing.
- Little storage space.
- Rather expensive when compared to the space available back.

CLASS C MOTORHOMES

Class C motorhomes are the middle of the road in the motorhome category. Also built on a van base, but only the front end has been retained. The rear part of the chassis has been completely redesigned and lengthened, widened and raised to accommodate the living area. Easily distinguishable by the bunk above the driver's cabin. About the same price range as the B class but with more space. It often has all the amenities of a home. Kitchen, bathroom, full bedroom, living room, TV, etc... It can also usually tow a smaller car than a class A motorhome.

Average length between 8M (23ft) and 13.5M (36ft)

Capacity for up to 8 people

Price range between 65000$ and 150 000$.

Benefits

- Most of the time, all the amenities.
- A home with a motor.
- More privacy most of the time at least one closed room.
- Despite the size, it does not require a special permit.
- Sets up quickly in the campground.
- Can often tow small vehicles.

Disadvantages

- Difficult to maneuver. Requires practice.
- For longer ones, more difficulty finding a campsite if not booked in advance.
- High weight causes high gas or diesel consumption.

THE TOWING VEHICLE AND THE HITCH

Understanding tow vehicles and how to hitch your RV.

Before you purchase the vehicle that will be used to tow your RV, make sure that it will be powerful enough to pull the load you will be putting on it. It is imperative to check the towing capacity of your vehicle if you do not want to have any surprises along the way.

To know the weight of the caravan that your towing vehicle can tow, refer to the manufacturer's recommendations. The information is usually written on the doorstop of the towing vehicle or in the owner's manual. If it is not, it is very easy to find it on the internet.

However, the towing capacity of your vehicle is not the law.

Did you know that the weight of your vehicle and the weight of your trailer with its contents must be considered when calculating the maximum towing capacity? You must not neglect what you are transporting, such as luggage, bicycles, water tanks, passengers, etc...

This extra weight will have an impact on the durability and handling of your vehicles. The more you move the maximum capacity, the greater the impact on the rear axle, tires, wheel bearings and brakes. You could end up on the side of the road or worse, have a serious accident. Don't forget that extra weight has an exponential effect on your vehicles ability to brake. If you do some research on the subject of towing capacity, you will most likely come across the following acronyms:

• **UVW: Unloaded Vehicle Weight.** This is the weight of your trailer unloaded and without additional equipment, so as it left the factory, to which is added the weights of the fluid tanks if they were at full capacity.

• **Dry Weight.** This is the weight of the caravan unloaded and without additional equipment, as it leaves the factory completely dry.

• **CCC: Gross Carrying Capacity or Cargo Capacity.** This is the maximum weight that can be loaded into your caravan without exceeding its GVWR.

• **GVW: Gross Vehicle Weight or GVW.** This is the total weight that your caravan will not exceed when fully loaded. In other words, the sum of the CCC and the UVW.

• **GTW: Gross Tiller Weight.** This is the same measurement as GVW, but it is specific to towed vehicles, whereas GVW can also apply to a motor vehicle.

• **GVWR: Gross Vehicle Weight Rating or GVWR, Gross Vehicle Weight Rating.** This is similar to GVW or GTW, it is the maximum weight your vehicle may not exceed.

• **GAWR: Gross Axle Weight Rating.** This is the maximum weight that can be supported by an axle.

• **Hitch Weight or Tiller Weight.** This is the portion of the trailer's weight that will rest on the tow vehicle's tongue. The proportion of this weight is normally around 10% to 15% of the weight (GVW or GTW) of the trailer or tent trailer and around 15% or 25% in the case of fifth wheel trailers.

• **Cargo weight.** Cargo weight is the actual weight of all items added to the empty weight of the vehicle or trailer. This includes personal cargo, optional equipment, and the weight of the boom or King Pin.

Keep in mind that the most important element is the GVWR or GVWR of each of your vehicles. First, how do you calculate this? You need to know the towing capacity of your vehicle.

For example, let's take a capacity of 2700kg (6000lbs). From this weight, you will have to deduct everything that is in your vehicle. Let's say 4 passengers for a total of 225kg (500lbs) and 90kg (200lbs) of luggage. The whole for a total of 315kg (700lbs). This weight must be subtracted from the towing capacity which is 2700kg (6000lbs) minus 315kg (700lbs). Therefore, the remaining capacity for your trailer will be 2385KG (5300LBS). This capacity must be greater than the GVWR or GVWR of your caravan. GVWR or GVWR being the maximum weight of your caravan. Of course, you must also make sure that the GVWR or GVWR of the caravan is respected.

Note that if your tow vehicle did not come from the factory with a tow package and you add one later, the towing capacity should not be considered as if it came from the factory with the tow package, but rather the vehicle without the tow package. The factory tow package will have a higher capacity because the manufacturer will take into account the overheating of the engine, the transmission and the braking capacity. Therefore, the towing package will not only include the drawbar at the rear but the radiator will be oversized, most likely the transmission will be equipped with a cooler and an improved braking capacity.

Towing capacity vs. trailer hitches.

There are several types of trailer hitches on the market. Here are a few of them and what they do.

The basic standard hitch has a ball and a fixed drawbar. It is suitable for lighter equipment such as micro-caravans and tent trailers.

The load sharing hitch has one or two tie bars, also called torsion bars, in addition to the ball and drawbar. The bars extend from each side of the front of the trailer. They support your towing vehicle by supporting it. The weight is distributed equally between the front and rear axle. The stability is optimized and the towing capacity is increased. Highly recommended for hybrid trailers or trailers even in some cases for heavy trailer tents. A sway bar can also be added as an option. This improves the stability and therefore the driving pleasure a little bit more.

The fifth wheel trailer hitch is usually designed with a rotating ball bearing. However, some hitches are equipped with one or more adjustable air cushions that reduce the impact that the truck transmits to the fifth wheel or vice versa.

Is there any other useful or useless equipment depending on your tow vehicle and your RV?

There are all kinds of equipment on the market to help with driving with a trailer. I give you my opinion on the usefulness of these equipment. From one RV to another, this equipment can be useful or not.

If your caravan is equipped with electric brakes, obviously it is essential to have a **controller for electric brakes**. Today, many vehicles, mostly pickup trucks, come from the factory with a built-in controller. If this is not the case and it is possible to have it as an option, I strongly suggest it because they are better adapted than those that are added after the purchase. Nevertheless, there are a variety of electric brake controllers from the low end to the high end.

The first selection criterion, choose your controller according to the weight you plan to pull. Indeed, not all controllers are made for the same use. There are ranges for 1 to 6 axles and a range of weights just as wide. Many, however, will do a wider range of weights or axles. Start by looking at controllers that are in your target range.

The second selection criterion is POD (power on demand) controllers. These are controllers that will apply the brakes in a more jerky fashion and will not take into account the speed you are traveling at when you apply the brakes. This is the low end of brake controllers as they apply the brakes unevenly but may be suitable for 1 or 2 axle equipment. Then there are the proportional controllers, these controllers are equipped with an accelerometer and apply the brakes according to the speed you are driving which gives a much more accurate and smooth braking. I would recommend that you do not neglect the controllers by choosing the lowest end of the range unless you do not travel very often or very far. These systems greatly improve your driving experience and stress.

The third selection criterion for the brake controller is whether you can buy a harness to fit your vehicle. You won't need to have a professional install your controller because with the right harness, it's very easy. If your vehicle has a good towing capacity and has the dealer's towing package option, chances are your vehicle already has a plug hidden under the dash near the pedals for you to plug in your controller. This makes it very easy to plug everything in within 5 minutes and saves you money on installation. Check in your vehicle's user guide or on the internet where this plug is located, what harness you will need and how to connect it.

With this information, you don't need a professional to do the installation and this is the best way to install it. Even if your vehicle doesn't have the tow package included, I suggest you check it out because there is a good chance that this plug exists.

The famous **wing on the roof** of the towing vehicle that is supposed to save you gas. You see where I'm going with this, well today's trailers are much more aerodynamic. Unless you have a trailer with a 90 degree front end like a 53 foot truck trailer, it's not useful at all, and in fact it could be the opposite and it will cost you more in gas. So forget about it.

Mirror extensions for your tow vehicle. There are a variety of different models. Honestly, I have never found one that fit 100% on my tow vehicle. Sometimes it took me forever to install it and once I did, when I was driving, it would move around, so I ended up giving up. At the limit it excites small concave mirrors that stick in the corner of your mirrors. It doesn't cost much and it does the job. 30 seconds to install and you only have to do it once.

A really useful gadget today, the **rear view camera**. You save a lot of time when you back up to hitch up your caravan and you can do it alone. If it's included in your vehicle, that's wonderful, if not, I recommend it. There are also wireless systems that you can install behind your trailer. I have one that I used for a while. It can be useful to see behind your RV when you are driving. Even when you are backing up with your RV.

A very useful piece of equipment that you rarely see are **suspension balloons**. These balloons are installed to support the suspension of your RV or tow vehicle. Large luxury RV's usually have them and they work like the ones on large transporters, adjusting automatically to the weight, so why not install them on your RV or tow vehicle? It greatly improves the ride by reducing sway.

Once installed, you add compressed air at equal pressure to each side. No need for an air compressor built right into the vehicle, it's perfectly possible to add pressure once at the beginning of your trip and remove the air only at the end of your trip. Some balloon models can be installed directly inside the vehicle's spring and do not cost much. If your suspension crashes a lot or there is a lot of wobble, this can be a great option.

Before you take your caravan on a long trip, what should you check?

The following list is a checklist of things you should check especially if you plan to do a lot of mileage. Check the things I am going to list at least a week in advance if possible. If there is ever a glitch, you will at least have time to fix it or have it fixed.

So, here are the things to check on your RV:

● Is the tire pressure good?

● Are the tires in good condition?

● The condition and pressure of your spare tire is often overlooked.

● Do you need to lubricate the wheel bearings?

● Is the propane full?

● Check the piping for leaks by putting it under water pressure especially after a winter.

● Electricity, lights and outlets, is everything working?

● Does the refrigerator work well?

● The battery holds its charge well?

● Following the winter, the roof has no apparent leaks? Roof, swollen wall or evidence of mold?

● Brake and turn signal lights work?

Remember, you will be working your tow vehicle hard by towing your RV. Your vehicle will require more force to move forward and the best thing to do is to give it everything it needs to do so as easily as possible. Here, I will give you more details since I will not go into much detail on the subject. **Things to check and do for your tractor or motorized vehicle. Why is this important?**

Check or change your engine and/or transmission oils as needed. If you have just changed your oils, you don't need to, but at least check the level and appearance. If your oil is black with carbon, well, change it. Over time the oil becomes less efficient so, more friction, more heat generation, more wear. We don't want that.

Make sure your radiator fins are not clogged with anything. Most of the time flies, butterflies, etc... We want to have the best heat release possible. Your vehicle will be working hard and giving off a lot of heat especially on hills so you need good heat exchange.

Do you have the right tires for towing? If you still have your winter tires, it's time to change them. Your winter tires may have a lower load rating than your summer tires and may not be designed to support the weight of your trailer. The load rating is usually listed after the tire size. For example: 185/70 R15 110H. The 110 represents the maximum load your tires can support when inflated to maximum pressure. In this case 110 means 1060KG. That's 1060KG per tire. If your vehicle is coming out of the dealership, it would be very surprising if you had a problem at this level. Manufacturers always supply tires that are well above the maximum full load weight (the GVWR or GVWR) of your vehicle. However, if you bought your vehicle used, I suggest you check if the owner before you was negligent in this aspect.

Are your tires inflated to the maximum recommended pressure and in good condition? A poorly inflated tire means more fuel consumption, premature wear and uneven driving.

Has your air filter been changed recently or is it clogged? Remember, your vehicle will be drawing in more air than usual to burn fuel properly so more air will pass through the filter. If your engine lacks air, the gasoline will be burned less efficiently and your engine will compensate by burning more gasoline, so it's worth it. Changing it is not very expensive and is the best solution.

Are your brakes in good condition? I don't need to tell you that your brakes will be used more than usual. When you have an extra weight to pull, good brakes make a big difference.

It's so much more fun to go with your head held high! In the next chapter, we're off at last!

DRIVING WITH AN RV

Driving an motorhome or trailer towed vehicle still requires some time to adapt and good reflexes. That's why it's important to adopt a safe driving style. Here are some practical tips to help you meet this challenge.

Before taking to the road with your RV, make sure you have the proper driver's license. Some countries, provinces or states require training when you exceed a certain trailer weight and others do not. Maybe by the time I write this the laws have changed so I won't get too involved. Whether you are allowed or not, it doesn't mean you shouldn't develop some driving habits. The longer your RV, the more you will need to develop your reflexes and observation skills. If you are intimidated by this idea, you should know that there are driving schools that offer theory and practical training for about half a day. Don't panic, it can be learned.

Be careful first. As you probably already know, it's easier to drive on a highway than to navigate city streets. In the city, you'll have the most difficulty adjusting. City streets are narrower and less welcoming to vehicles that need a lot of room to move. Because your vehicle is heavier, acceleration and especially braking will take longer, so keep your distance and get in the habit of slowing down ahead of time. The faster you drive, the longer your braking distance will be.

Also, the large size of your RV will make it more sensitive to wind.

Wind gusts are sometimes not very pleasant. Keeping a reasonable cruising speed will make your ride more enjoyable. Keep in mind that you will also generate more turbulence and be more susceptible to turbulence from other cars. In particular, large cargo trailers. When you are overtaken by a vehicle or when a vehicle overtakes you, there is a break in the turbulence that is created at a certain point. This causes your vehicle and the one next to you to tend to want to get closer together. It is not a pull effect but rather the turbulence still existing on the other side that pushes your vehicle. The larger your trailer and the faster you drive, the more you will feel this effect.

Have you ever seen a semi-truck drive over the curb? You can expect the same challenges when learning the mechanics of turning with your RV. One of the things most often forgotten when driving with a trailer or motorhome is that you will need more room to turn. When fully loaded, you will need more braking distance and a wider turning radius, especially when making right turns. For a trailer in particular, it is often forgotten that the pivot point of the trailer is not the same as the tow vehicle. What is the best travel trailer turning trick? Before you turn your RV around, you'll need to give yourself extra room to steer through the intersection before you begin the turn. This is known as the "pull straight, turn late" method. When driving your RV, you will need to consider your trailer's tires when making turns, primarily to the right. You will need to go further into the intersection than you are used to before you start making your turn. Hence the phrase; shoot straight, turn late. If you don't, your trailer's wheels could ride up on the sidewalk or worse, you could hit something on the corner like a pole or a car.

Don't forget to consider the tail of your RV when turning. The tail is the area between the rear bumper and the pivot point. The tail can be large enough to move into the next lane during a turn. This can lead to a car accident or worse, hitting a pedestrian if you are not careful. The greater the distance between the rear wheels and the rear bumper of your RV, the greater the tail swing. It's essential to consider tail swing when driving by anything with your RV, such as other cars, gas pumps, pedestrians, street signs, and even hookups at a campground. As you can see in the following diagram, the truck's tail swings to the left when making a right turn, creating a potential for an accident.

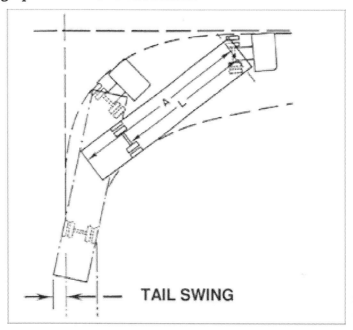

TAIL SWING

With a trailer attached, your blind spots will be more pronounced. If a vehicle tries to pass you on the highway, you will lose sight of it for a moment, hence the importance of being attentive at all times. If your RV is quite large, take a good look at the height and width signs, especially in construction zones and toll booths. Now these famous signs will speak to you too. Be careful of branches and wires and before you enter a lane that seems cramped, make sure you'll get out of it unscathed at the other end. Getting back on track once you've started with an RV is rather complex.

The goal here is not to discourage you at all, it can be learned like riding a bike. Before you head out on your adventure, why don't you do a little practice around the area in places you know? It's less stressful to get started.

How To Adjust Your Electric Brakes?

First of all, when you take your RV out after a long time in storage, you may have some rust on the brakes. They will slip a little more on the first few stops. This is normal, don't panic. You may wonder why it doesn't brake well. Once the rust is gone, it's time to adjust your brakes. For the best ride, adjust your brakes slightly more on your trailer than on your vehicle. It's better to feel held back than pushed back when braking.

How to adjust? If your controller is built into your vehicle by the manufacturer, it will have a small control panel somewhere with an emergency brake button. Consult your owner's manual. Otherwise, get a controller according to the criteria I discussed in part #2 of the book. All modules have at least one wheel or knob to adjust the tension and a button for emergency braking. To adjust your brakes, play with the adjustment wheel or knobs until you find the perfect position. Note the location of the emergency button. Look in the manual if you have to, to be sure, because you may need it and by the time you get it out, it will be too late. This button is mainly used when you are going down a very steep slope and all of a sudden you realize that the adjustment you took the trouble to make is not correct at all. Instead of taking the time to readjust everything during your rather stressful descent, you hit the emergency button. Usually this button is variable like a spring. The harder you push it, the more it brakes. It could save your life.

RV TRAVELLER'S GUIDE

Backing Up With Your Rv

Backing up with your RV is not so easy. It can be frustrating, nerve-wracking, and leave you sweating. The first thing to remember is to take your time and breathe. Like everyone else, I wasn't a pro the first time and several times after. It takes practice. The best thing is to keep your cool. I know it's easy to say, but it's the best thing you can do. Don't worry about all the stares and people who seem impatient. If you have a chance, let them pass and continue on your way. To back up with a large motorhome, you have to plan for the larger space it takes to turn. Other than that, it's the same principle as a standard vehicle but with a long trailer, it's different.

How do you handle the steering wheel? When you turn around and back up, the trailer and tow vehicle form a V shape away from the direction you are turning. As you move forward, the V will become more and more distinct if you hold the wheel still. The more dramatically you turn the wheel, the sharper the angle becomes. Go too hard, and you can get a pocket knife. You'll want to avoid that!

A little trick to help you know where your trailer will go, with your hand at the bottom of your steering wheel, the direction you move your hand is the direction the end of your trailer will go as you back up. If you need to straighten up, the best way to do so is to move forward, not backward. It is difficult, if not impossible, to straighten out backwards when the trailer is well underway in one direction. Ideally, steer your wheels toward the direction you want the trailer to go and keep doing this until you are aligned. Whenever you feel stuck, moving forward and trying to straighten out is almost always your best option. To get back to your original position, move forward as much as possible. This will give you enough room to get the right angle to back up.

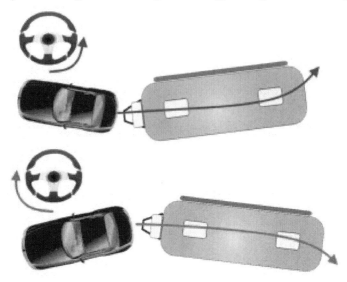

Do yourself a favor and practice in a large open parking lot before trying to go back to a campsite. The best way to learn is to practice. If you already have your trailer, drive it to a large open parking lot in your area where there is no risk. There, you can practice turning as you please to get a real feel for how it works. It might also be a good idea to bring traffic cones or other obstacles that won't hurt your trailer to simulate backing into a campsite.

The golden rule, stay calm. Go slowly and don't panic. You can always take a few seconds to stop, catch your breath and try again. Many RV veterans know how you feel. They've been in your shoes. They may even offer help and advice, so be sure to listen with both ears and write down everything they tell you.

Managing Your Gas Tank

I go back to my formula mentioned in how to choose your RV chapter (as an indication).

According to a study (U.S. departement of energy), each 100kg(220lbs) is equivalent to about 0,5L/100km or each 100lbs(45kg) is equivalent to 1% less mpg(miles per gallon):

Consumption L/100KM for a weight of 2200kg(+/- 5000lbs):

2200kg/100kg = 22

22 x 0.5L/100km = 11L/100km to add for your caravan or total weight of your motorhome

Or in mpg

Consumption MPG for a weight of 5000lb(+/- 2200kg):

5000lbs/100 = 50

50 x 1% = 50%

For a vehicle consuming 23mpg : 23mpg - 50% = 11.5mpg

This is an estimate, many other factors come into play but it gives you a good starting point.

Mountain Driving.

Most newly manufactured vehicles for towing have a button to manage driving with a trailer or your motorhome is already designed for it. The engine runs faster, more power available, better lubrication and cooling, the transmission will heat up less. Less shifting, less hesitation between gears. It will be easier to manage.

When driving on the smaller hills, it's at least energy management. As much as possible you try to take advantage of a descent to attack the next climb. Nothing happens on the way down unless you immediately get to the bottom, let it accelerate and secure to get back up. No unnecessary wear of the brakes, less fuel consumed, less effort the mechanics. So far, it's not too complicated.

On longer climbs, where it is obvious that you will not be able to climb all the way to the top thanks to the momentum, you have to accept the decrease in speed and let the horse breathe. There is no point in trying to go up the hill at 90 km/h. With experience, you will find the ideal engine speed for climbing. You will feel the maximum power of the engine at this speed. There is no point in running the engine at very high speed just to get to the top 10 seconds faster...

For long descents, it is imperative to keep control of the speed and not to overheat the brakes. Keep a constant pressure on the brakes vs. braking and releasing, I am a proponent of the intermittent braking technique, that is to say a good braking to slow down and then a pause to let the brakes cool down. In my opinion, constant pressure on the brakes until the bottom of the hill is to be avoided and can result in overheating of the brakes and loss of control. But not everyone agreed with me.

On very long descents, try to plan your approach. I strongly recommend engine braking like the large trailers used. If your vehicle is recent and you have a towing button, it is very likely that this management will be done by itself. If not, and despite this option, before you even start down this kind of road, I strongly advise you to visualize the actions you will take. Find out where the manual gears are. On my truck for example, they are on the steering wheel. Know how many gears you have, too. When approaching a long, steep descent, select the manual mode and shift down manually so that it is the engine rather than the brakes that slows your descent. I also suggest that you do some test runs to get a feel for the engine's rpm in different gears. During a steep descent, this is not really the right time. You need to slow down and manually select a lower gear before it starts to go downhill, otherwise it may be impossible to slow down enough to do so. The steeper it is, the lower gear you select. I have ridden through the rocky mountains in Canada with an RV and I can tell you that this technique is paramount and even vital. The hills sometimes descend in an "S" shape and it is impossible to take a curve at more than 20km/h. If you master this technique, it will be a piece of cake. This is exactly the same technique used by semi-trailers. It is the Jacob brake principle. On vacation we are not in a hurry so abuse it if you have to.

THE DEVICES IN YOUR RV. HOW THEY WORK AND HOW TO SERVICE OR REPAIR THEM

This part of the book is a guide to the operation and maintenance of the various devices in your RV. This is not a mechanic's guide, but is for anyone who wants to know how the various devices in your RV work and how to service or repair them. After reading this part, you should be able to know how your appliances work and do most of the maintenance.

Hopefully, with this guide, you will learn more about the operation and maintenance of your RV and be better able to prevent electrical and mechanical problems. By knowing how the various devices in your RV work, you will be better able to diagnose and repair problems. Even if you decide not to do the repairs yourself, you will be in a better position to deal with your repairman.

When you're away from it all with your RV, a guide like this can be a great help and will give you peace of mind.

THE EXTENSIONS

Before opening the extensions, it is important to make sure that your RV is level because you could damage the walls and make the motors work for nothing. Before opening, make sure that there is enough room on the outside to open the extension. Press the "OUT" button until the extension is fully open. When done, remove your finger from the button as soon as you can so as not to force the motors. Same thing when you close. When closing the extension, always make sure that you are level and that there are no obstructions on the inside, such as a drawer or door, on the top and outside, such as branches, that could get caught and damage your RV. Once everything is checked, press the "IN" button to close the extension.

There are several types of extension mechanisms, but they can be grouped into 3 main types. The first and most commonly used type is **the electric or hydraulic sliding tube type**.

No matter, the principle is basically the same, it's just the way the power is transmitted to move the extension out or in that changes. Some have motors with a serrated wheel and a serrated rod like the picture above. Easy to recognize because of the apparent serrated rods. This mechanism usually has a motor on each synchronized tube that pushes or pulls the tube.

The motors are located under the RV, often hidden from view to protect it from debris. Easy to recognize by the serrated rods. The teeth of the rod should be lubricated occasionally with a dry lubricant, such as "WD40", to prevent dust and debris from sticking to them. Spray lubricant liberally on all components that are in motion. Gears, tubes, anything that rubs or slides.

If you have a breakdown, check the fuses first. If you want to move the extension in or out, there should be a gear system to do it manually with a wrench.

Under the extension, near the frame, there is a square rod with 2 cogwheels connected to the cogwheels. The square rod is parallel to the frame. With an adjustable wrench or the right size wrench, you can turn the square rod to move the extension in or out.

In the same type with sliding tube, there are some with electric cylinders and worm screw. There is also a tube system but it is a worm screw jack that moves the extension in or out. In some cases, there is also the manual system with gears as before to move the extension in or out.

You will also need dry lubricant to service the auger. Spray all moving parts generously with lubricant. Sights, tubes, anything that rubs or slides. The motor is also located under the RV, probably hidden under a protective cover on the sight.

In case of failure, if there is a cover, remove it, if not, you will have to make a hole about the same distance from the chassis as your extension extended to its maximum. If the extension comes out 90cm (36") from the chassis, the motor should be about 90cm (36") from the chassis towards the inside. A square hole of about 30cm (12") should be sufficient. Locate the motor and the motor gear. On the gear you should see a rod or a hexagonal nut. With a wrench, you can turn the gear back and forth to move the extension in or out.

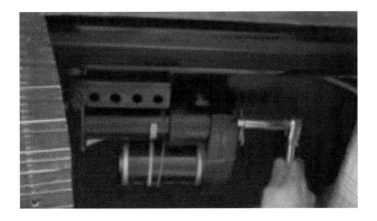

However, if it is the gear that fails, you will have to remove the mechanism to get the extension in by pushing it.

It also has the traction systems with cable and pulley. You can also easily locate them under the extension. As before, all moving parts, pulley, tubes will need to be lubricated with dry lubricant. The motor can be hidden under a cover inside the caravan at floor level or on top.

Remove the cover to gain access to the motor. You will see the motor and cable system. On the motor and gear, there should be a hex hole where you can insert a hex adapter. With an electric drill connected to this hex adapter, you can turn the mechanism to move the extension in or out. You may need a flexible adapter to fit the hex adapter if the space is too small.

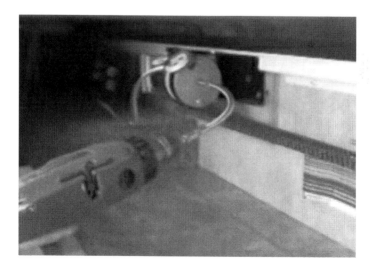

The Second Most Common Type Is The System With Rails At The 4 Corners.

Each rail has its own motor that synchronizes together to move the extension in and out. This is, in my opinion, the simplest and easiest system to maintain. The rails will occasionally need to be lubricated with a dry lubricant. The motors are accessible from the inside or outside of the trailer in the four corners where the rails are located. To access them, you would have to remove the cover or moldings. The motor is fairly simple to remove. Most of the time, it will only need to be removed by hand and a new one put back in with almost no tools.

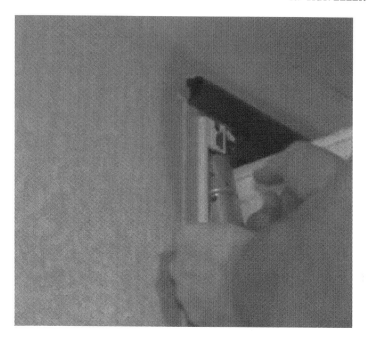

In case of a failure, first check the motor controller which is probably hidden somewhere behind a cover inside. Check the user's manual. Once found, if a light is blinking, you can reset it by pressing the "reset" button.

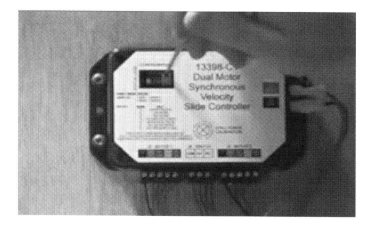

If the controller does not reset or a motor is defective, unplug both motor connectors and simply push the extension in the desired direction.

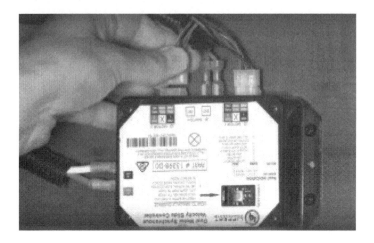

The third type is the hydraulic system. Mainly on fifth wheel caravans or more luxurious motorhomes. The system works with slide tubes but the driving force is one or more hydraulic cylinders operated by an electric pump. Most of the time the hydraulic pump is located at the front with a small oil tank that should be checked from time to time. The pump sends oil into the cylinders to move the extension in and out.

If the motor stops working, in most cases you can operate the hydraulic pump with an Allen wrench style hex adapter and a drill.
If you don't have a hex rod, install any adapter rod (star, flat, what-
ever) upside down on your drill so you only have the hex end. Remove the cap on top of the motor and insert the hex adapter into
the hole where the cap was. Rotate the motor with your drill in
either direction to move the extension in or out.

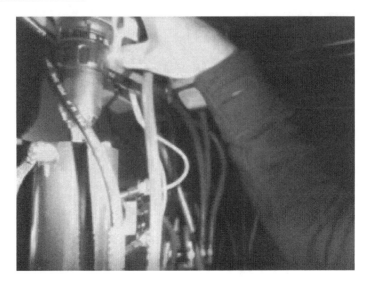

This is a grouping of the main mechanical extension systems. Even if you don't find exactly the same system, the principle is the same and you will be able to do the maintenance and repair yourself.

THE AIR CONDITIONING SYSTEM

Nowadays, almost all camping vehicles are equipped with air conditioners. Since RV's are mainly used in the summer in hot weather, comfort depends mainly on the air conditioning, so it is essential to make sure it is working properly. RV air conditioners work exactly the same way as residential air conditioners. Some systems have ducted air distribution systems inside the RV, while others are ductless, and the cool air comes directly from the system to the roof. Some also have a wall mounted thermostat and some directly on the air conditioner. Regardless, the system is exactly the same. I am not going to give you a course in thermodynamics, the purpose of the following diagram is to explain the basic principle so that you understand the importance of maintenance and avoid unnecessary service calls.

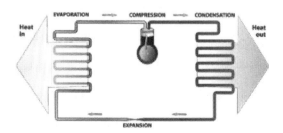

We are interested in the two heat exchangers. For the rest, you will probably need the services of a refrigeration technician. The first heat exchanger is located inside called the evaporator. This one recovers the heat that is pumped out by the compressor and sends it to the outside exchanger, called the condenser, to reject the heat. Here you have the basis. For the heat exchange to work properly, the exchangers must be cleaned because dust and debris act as an insulator. The more the accumulation becomes, the less efficient the exchanger becomes and your system will end up accumulating heat which could damage the other components. In my opinion, at least 50% of service calls are the result of this maintenance neglect.

The frequency of maintenance of heat exchangers depends on your use. If you only use your RV in the summer for a few weeks, once a year will probably be sufficient. The interior heat exchanger or evaporator is often the one that accumulates the least amount of dust. This doesn't mean you shouldn't do maintenance on it, but it will be easier. First, make sure to turn off the power to your air conditioning system so that you don't hurt yourself or damage the system during maintenance. Then the ceiling grid on the inside. You may have to remove the knob or screws. Underneath the grill, there should be a small foam filter. This filter will need to be cleaned. Clean it with a vacuum cleaner or wash it in the sink with dish soap. If the filter is too damaged, replace it. Check for dust accumulation in the opening before replacing the filter and screen. If there is, use a vacuum cleaner to remove the dust.

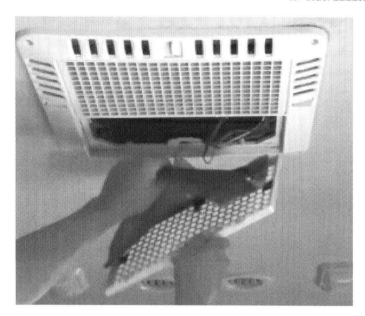

For the outdoor exchanger, the condenser, you will have to climb on the roof. Again, make sure the power is off. Remove the cover of the air conditioner. As there are several different models, check the user's manual to see how to remove the cover. In some models, the cover is held on by screws and in others by clips. Regardless, it is certain that the cover can be removed. Clean the exchanger or condenser first with a vacuum cleaner and then I advise you to send compressed air to dislodge the dust caught deeper. Once you have blown the air out, vacuum the condenser again. Also, take the opportunity to vacuum the entire system. Dust and debris on the compressor, fan motor and fin are also damaging in the long run.

If your air conditioner is really dirty, there are soaps available specifically for condensers. Check with your dealer.

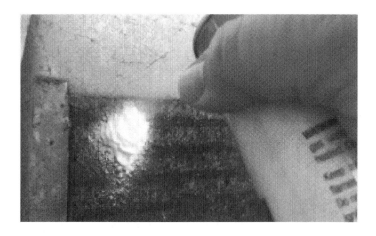

The more regular maintenance you do on your air conditioner, the easier it will be to do. If you leave the dust around too long, it will eventually harden and be harder to remove.

Next, check that the condenser fins are straight. Bent fins again reduce heat exchange and thus the efficiency of your air conditioner. There are tools specifically designed to do this job, or you can simply use a pocket knife to straighten them.

Now that the maintenance is done, you can replace the cover, turn on the power and use your air conditioner. Check that the heat exchange is done inside your RV. The temperature difference between the room air and the outlet should be about 10oc to 15oc. Obviously, this can vary greatly depending on the humidity level and the speed at which the air passes through the evaporator. This is just a guideline but there is no exact number.

HOW THE ELECTRICAL SYSTEM AND THE BATTERY WORK

Electrical power comes from two sources, 12 volts from the battery and 120 volts. When your RV is plugged into a 120 volt outlet, the 12 volt appliances are powered by the power converter. The power converter is actually a transformer that lowers the current from 120 volts to 12 volts. All the devices working on 12 volts are protected by fuses like those used in cars. The 120 volt current is protected by circuit breakers like those used in a home.

The following drawing shows the 30 Amp and 50 Amp outlets to help you in case of troubleshooting.

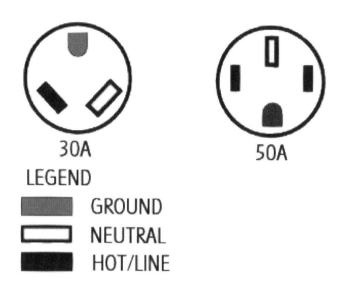

30A   50A

LEGEND

GROUND
NEUTRAL
HOT/LINE

When your RV is not plugged into a 120 volt circuit, only 12 volt appliances will work. **Here is a list of appliances that work on 12 volts:**

• Lights

• Refrigerator

• Heating system

• Hot water tank

• Water pump

• Bathroom fan

• Gas detector

• 12-volt outlet

All of these appliances can run on 12 volts or a combination of

12 volts and propane gas such as the refrigerator, heating system and hot water tank. For these three appliances, only the controls and fan work on 12 volts. The heat comes from the propane gas burner. We will see it in the sections reserved for these devices.

When your RV is plugged in the appliances running on 120 volts can work:

• Microwave oven

• Air conditioner

• Television and audio system (Some appliances can also operate on 12 volts)

• Power converter

• Hot water tank if your hot water tank has a heating element.

Here is a typical RV circuit diagram to help you understand:

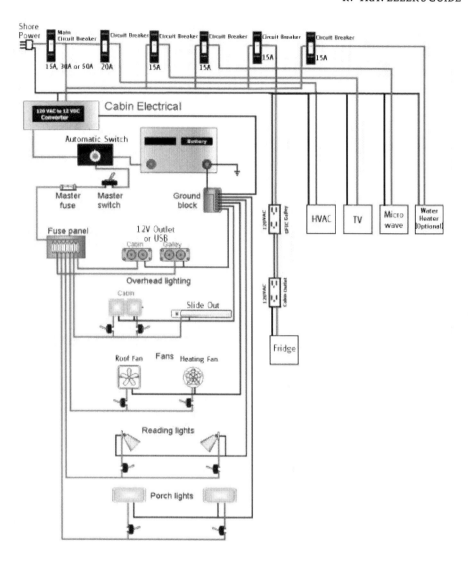

Obviously, this diagram is not necessarily the one for your trailer but it should be close. As you can see from the diagram, when you plug in on 120 volts, the converter, in most cases today, automatically takes its power source on 120 volts to save your battery. Today, most converters automatically recharge your battery when you plug in. Your RV battery will also be recharged by your vehicle's alternator when you drive.

If you are planning to go wilderness camping, you will probably need a good battery if you are not going to be plugged into your vehicle or a 120 volt circuit for any length of time. Most RVs can accommodate two or more batteries. You will have the choice between two 12 volt batteries or two 6 volt batteries. However, the connection will not be the same. For two 12 volt batteries, you will have to connect them in parallel and the 6 volt batteries will have to be connected in series to have 12 volts.

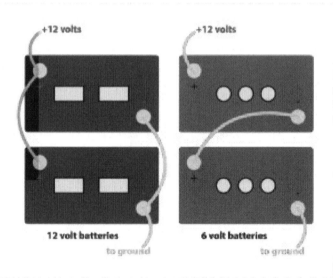

Among the different types of batteries, it is the deep cycle battery, also called "marine battery" that you need. This battery is often compared to a car battery because of its size, but its use is not the same!

The deep cycle battery is designed to provide power over a long period of time, to run lights and other 12 volt equipment for several hours. So it provides a certain number of amps per hour.

A car battery can give almost all its power, in one big burst, to run a starter motor at full speed, and then be recharged by the alternator. This battery can be drained very quickly if constant current is required. (For ex: A forgotten light).

Contrary to what one may think, the term deep discharge can mislead many people. People often think that it is a battery that can be completely and deeply discharged. But in fact it is the "amperage reserve" that is deep and has more autonomy. This type of battery can be seriously damaged if you discharge it completely. So, your best bet is to conserve its charge as much as possible.

To keep your battery healthy for many years, I recommend never going below 50% (12.28V) of its capacity and charging it with a proper charger. In other words, try to keep your battery fully charged at all times. You will save battery cycles, extend the life of your battery and make recharging easier. A battery that is too discharged will not easily recover.

Choose your battery capacity carefully if you want it to last as long as possible without recharging. The higher the amperage/hour (e.g. 250AH), the longer it will last. Usually a 6-volt battery for the same capacity as a 12-volt will cost less.

It is quite possible that your RV is equipped with a level monitor. The level monitor will help you, among other things, to make sure that you do not lower the charge level of your battery too much. The level monitor also has a level indicator for your fresh water, gray water and black water tanks if you have them. The fresh water tank pump button is most likely on there as well. Here is a typical picture of a level monitor:

When you press one of the buttons, it shows you the level of that button. It often happens that the level monitor displays wrong data, especially for grey and black water. It is possible to bring them back. This is often due to the fact that the tanks are too dirty.

Use a degreasing cleaner with hot water and put 2 good pails in each tank and drive away with your RV. During the road, the movement stirs it all up and when you arrive at your destination, you change the oil and often the indicators are back to normal. Do this 2 or 3 times during the season. It eliminates, at the same time, the odors and prevents eventual blocking problems. Ideally, it should be done at temperatures above 24°C (76°F). Fats are more soluble above this temperature.

If you have a problem with one of your 12-volt appliances or lights, check the following things:

• Is your battery properly connected and recharged?

Check your level monitor, if you have one, to see how much charge the battery has. If your indicator shows nothing at all, check to see if your battery is plugged in and working. If you have any doubts about the condition of your battery, remove it and try to recharge it with a suitable charger. It often happens that a battery gives an indication of charge but as soon as you give it a charge, the voltage drops, so it is necessary to check it with a device designed for this purpose. To avoid complicating your life and buying unnecessary equipment, take your battery to a specialized battery store or to your dealer. If your monitor indicates full charge, proceed to the next step.

• However, it would be normal for your battery monitor to indicate full charge if your RV is plugged into a 120 volt outlet even if the battery is discharged so check this.

• Your battery shows full charge and your device(s) still does not work then check the fuses.

• Check the main fuse first if all 12 volt appliances are not working. Replace as needed but before doing so, ask yourself what could have caused the fuse to burn out so it doesn't happen again before replacing.

• If only one of the 12-volt devices does not work, the steps seen before will probably not be necessary. Check the fuse on that unit. The location of the fuse should be identified. Before replacing the fuse, check to see what may have caused the fuse to burn out before replacing. First make a visual inspection and refer to the section for this device in the book you are holding.

• A blown fuse will appear blackened when you look at it but sometimes it is difficult to distinguish if they are actually blown so instead of inspecting it every which way, with a magnifying glass and your reading glasses, just replace it anyway and verify that your appliance in question is working properly.

If one or more of your 120-volt outlets is no longer working, here are the things to check.

• Check that the circuit breaker on the panel you plugged in from has not tripped. If the breaker has tripped, check with the chart below to help you check for too many appliances working simultaneously.

• If in doubt, you can still check that the outlet you plugged in from is functional with a pilot light or other appliance running on 120 volts. If it is a 30 or 50 amp outlet, you will need a millimeter to check the voltage.

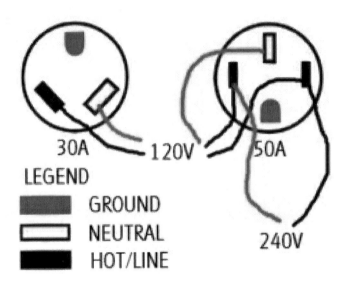

30A — 120V — 50A

LEGEND

■	GROUND
□	NEUTRAL
■	HOT/LINE

240V

• Check that the wire connecting the caravan to the outlet is properly connected and functional.

• Check that the "reset" button on the GFIC socket, probably located in the bathroom, has not been tripped. Press "test" first and then "reset".

• Check the main circuit breaker on the trailer electrical panel has not tripped.

• If only one outlet or appliance does not work, check the circuit breaker supplying that appliance. Before resetting the circuit breaker, check to see what may have caused the circuit breaker to trip. Check the condition of the appliance.

• Check with a lamp, for example, that the socket to which this appliance is connected is actually powered.

• If after all these steps your 120 volt appliance still does not work, check that your appliance is working properly by plugging it into another outlet.

If the problem is with the circuit breaker on the panel you plugged in from, check to see if your problem is caused by running too many appliances at once. If you are plugged into a 30 amp breaker, check that the sum of all your appliances that were running at the same time does not exceed 30 amps.

Here is a small table showing the consumption of certain appliances.

19-inch television	1 amp
1 amp	1 amp
Refrigerator 120 volts 3ft3 (Excluding gas)	1.5 amps
Coffee maker 9 amps	12 amps
Microwave	15 amps
Air conditioner	15 amps
Hair dryer maximum	12 amps
Vacuum cleaner	11 amps
Electric heating elements hot water tank	13 amps

PROPANE GAS
INSTALLATIONS

Propane gas is stored in your tanks in its liquid form. In its liquid form, propane looks like water but unlike water, its boiling point at atmospheric pressure is -42oc (-44of). For propane to be in its liquid form in your tanks, the pressure must rise to 140 PSI at a temperature of 21oc(70of). Since propane gas is stored in its liquid form in a sealed tank and in its gaseous form it takes up much more space, it is the pressure inside that will vary with temperature. So the higher the temperature, the higher the pressure. The tanks are designed to withstand the pressure.

U.S. law requires that all cylinders must be inspected and requalified, or replaced, every ten years. The date on the neck of the cylinder indicates the last requalification. Only a qualified person may fill your cylinder. An attendant is not allowed to fill an expired cylinder or fill a cylinder to more than 80% of its capacity. All regulatory tanks today are equipped with devices that limit filling above 80%. Propane cylinders and tanks must be equipped with a safety valve that opens and closes to prevent excessive internal pressure caused by abnormal conditions.

Propane vapor is more than 1.5 times heavier than air. For this reason, propane gas detectors are installed at ground level. Gas detectors are mandatory in all recreational vehicles since 1996. In many cases, the detectors are even connected to an electric solenoid valve located upstream that shuts off the gas supply in case of a leak. Moreover, if your gas appliances do not work, it is perhaps because this valve is closed. It is an almost odorless gas. An odorous substance, ethylmercaptan, is added to it to give it an odor similar to rotten eggs or sulfur. The purpose, as you probably know, is to make it easier to detect. A drop in power can also trigger a false alarm. One way to check that your gas detector is working properly is to place a butane lighter near it without lighting it. However, the best thing to do is to check the manufacturer's specifications.

If you detect a leak, you should:

• Extinguish all flames, pilot lights and burning objects.

• Do not touch electrical switches as they can create a spark sufficient to start a fire.

• Turn off gas taps or supplies.

• Open doors and windows.

• Leave the room until you can no longer smell the odor.

• Once dissipated, have the gas system checked and repaired by a qualified technician.

If you still want to detect the leak yourself, the best method is still a mixture of a little water with soap. Use a non-corrosive soap such as dish soap. Dip a small brush into the soap or use a bottle with a spray nozzle to brush it onto the pipes you suspect are defective. If it bubbles, you've found your problem. There are sprayers available for purchase in stores, but in my opinion, soap and water is all you need. Depending on the problem you find, tighten the adapter or replace the defective part.

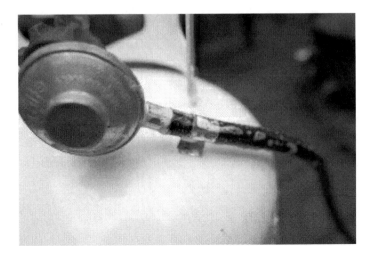

A pressure regulator is installed immediately after the gas outlet of the propane cylinder, after the valve.

The purpose of the regulator is to lower the gas pressure to a pressure suitable for your RV appliances. The pressure is not adjustable and the pressure is usually very low, under 1 PSI, so it is difficult to measure. He makes sure that the air intake of the regulator is well cleaned.

It could happen that ice forms inside the regulator if water mixes with the propane gas. The pressure will be reduced or completely shut off. To solve the problem, you can, for example, pour a bottle of hot water over the regulator. The heat will melt the ice and the flow will be restored. If the regulator freezes, it could be because the air intake is dirty, your bottle is overfilled or there is water in the bottle.

There are automatic changeover regulators like this one:

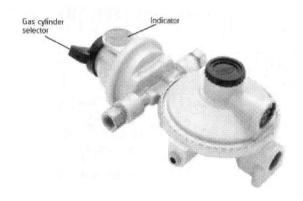

Today, most RVs with two cylinders have this type of regulator. The automatic changeover feature allows you to have a constant supply of gas in your system. If the selected cylinder is empty, the regulator will draw gas from the other cylinder without you noticing. The color of the indicator will change from green to red indicating that the selected cylinder is empty. Before disconnecting the empty cylinder, turn the lever toward the cylinder that is now the primary cylinder. The indicator will turn green and you can disconnect your empty bottle and have it filled. It is very important to turn the lever before disconnecting the empty cylinder as gas may escape from the removed hose.

THE FRESH WATER SUPPLY SYSTEM

The fresh water system is one of the most popular systems in RVs. Despite what you may think, it is quite easy to maintain. The most common system in RVs today is the 12-volt pump system that circulates water through the system when a faucet is turned on. Most RV's are equipped with a polyethylene tank, a light, durable, resistant and hygienic material. Some luxury RVs have stainless steel tanks. Their size often varies according to the occupancy capacity of the RV. They rarely exceed 50 gallons because the amount of water that gets tossed around on the road exerts considerable pressure.

Maintaining the fresh water tank is fairly simple, take a quarter cup of homemade bleach for every 15 liters of water your fresh water tank holds. Mix the bleach with water in a one gallon (or 4 liter) container and pour it into the fresh water tank. Fill the fresh water tank at least halfway before you take your RV on the road. The motion will clean your tank properly. When you arrive at your destination, circulate the water throughout your water system with the pump to thoroughly clean and disinfect the system. Drain excess water from the fresh water tank using the drain valve, which is sometimes located inside if you have access to your tank from the inside, otherwise it will be located under your RV. In some cases, there will be no valve but a cap, so remove the cap. Properly flush the tank and fresh water system with new water.

If you have **a leak on your fresh water tank**, it can be repaired with epoxy and fiberglass. First:

• Completely drain tank and dry out the entire area around the crack or hole. If the crack is inaccessible, you will unfortunately have to remove the tank.

• If it is a crack, drill a hole about 1/8 inch (0.3 cm) at each end of the crack. This will prevent the crack from continuing to grow after the tank is repaired.

• Sand the surface around the crack or hole as necessary to allow the resin to adhere properly.

• Cut a piece of fiberglass wider and longer than the crack by at least 1 inch (2.5 cm).

• Make your epoxy resin mixture as directed by the resin manufacturer.

• With a brush, apply a first coat of epoxy resin on the sanded surface and put your fiberglass piece.

• Reapply a layer of epoxy resin so that your fiberglass piece is completely soaked and the fiberglass is completely smooth.

• The surface should be dry to the touch after 30 minutes but wait 24 hours before putting water back in your tank.

If the crack is major, it is possible to have it welded by a plastic welding specialist. Of course, if your tank is made of stainless steel, it is also possible to have it welded by a competent technician.

Fresh water systems in RV's today are almost all made of PEX plastic pipe. This pipe is easy to install because of its flexibility and does not require welding. In addition, it can expand if there is still water in it when the temperature drops below zero and the water freezes. This does not mean, however, that you should not winterize your caravan for the winter.

You will have to check from time to time that the connections are tight, especially when your RV is new. Vibration and movement on the road can loosen the fittings and create leaks. Sometimes, there may be a leak but you can't see it. A good way to know if there is a leak in your system is to leave all the faucets closed and then leave the water pump on. If it starts up every once in a while and you don't turn on a faucet, there is a leak somewhere and you need to find it because it could seriously damage your RV.

If the fresh water pump does not prime, it is probably sucking air. Make sure that the fittings at the pump inlet are tight, the pump will suck in air and this will interfere with proper operation. Of course, first make sure that the fresh water tank is sufficiently full because the pump will run continuously. A pump that runs without water for too long can become damaged. The components inside will overheat, since they will not be cooled by water, and will burn out, so a good habit is to check the inlet fittings and make sure the pump is still drawing water. You may have a filter at the pump inlet to prevent the pump from drawing in debris. It will need to be cleaned from time to time to ensure that the pump is doing its job. If not, I suggest you install one because otherwise your pump could suck in debris and be damaged.

Most RV's can be connected, with a water hose, to a water outlet either from your home or from campgrounds with a fresh water service. This will save you a lot of water from your fresh water tank. I strongly suggest that you use a white garden hose like the ones sold at RV dealerships. The reason is that the white color attracts less sunlight and the water will taste better. In addition, these hoses are designed and approved for consumption.

There are several types of water filters on the market that can be installed on your fresh water inlet.

Water filters are used to capture deposits and particles in the water and to remove odors to give the water a better taste. Filters are disposable and should be replaced at least once a year. When the filter is blocked, you will notice that the pressure and circulation decreases or worse, it may start to reject the particles it had previously captured. When the filter has had a full season, it is best to replace it.

Another good practice is to install a pressure regulator at the water inlet of your RV. Some campgrounds maintain too much water pressure which can cause leaks in your water system. A good way to avoid this is to install a pressure regulator. There are several types and qualities available, but no matter what you choose, prevention is better than cure.

THE WASTE WATER SYSTEM

Most RV manufacturers agree on the same wastewater recovery system. On the one hand, you have a black water tank that collects the waste water from the toilets and on the other hand, another tank to collect the grey water which is the water from the sinks, sinks and bath/shower. The outlet of these two tanks is usually connected together and the water is both retained by a drain valve. Some larger models even have two grey water tanks that are not necessarily connected together.

Before all this, you will have to maintain your toilet. There are a variety of models and functions but basically you have the fresh water toilet, the recycled water toilet, the portable toilet or the dry toilet. The most common model is the freshwater toilet. The fresh water toilet uses either water from the fresh water tank or water from your outdoor connection if you are connected with a hose. Depending on your model, the toilet is either pedal-operated or a hand lever is used to send the waste into the black water storage tank. A jet of water cleans your toilet when it is activated. Many toilet models have two levers or two levels on the same lever that allow you to put water in the toilet before using it. Of course, there are more and less luxurious toilets, but they work in a similar way. Some models even have a flush hose to clean the tank after use. Most of the time, they are made of plastic but some models are made of ceramic and even stainless steel.

In the **portable toilet**, you have your seat with a flapper also at the bottom of the bowl, a fresh water tank that is often directly under the seat and the waste water tank completely underneath. This type of toilet is often found in tent trailers and their tanks can be emptied like other tanks with a wastewater valve on the outside. When the toilet is flushed, the fresh water in the top tank is used to clean the tank to facilitate flushing into the wastewater tank. Very similar to the fresh water toilet only the tank is above ground rather than hidden under the RV.

The recycled water model is the same function as a portable toilet except that it does not have a fresh water supply but rather uses a system that filters and reuses the flushed water. When the toilet is flushed, a pump draws water from the wastewater tank through a filter and the water is recycled. The flushing system is the same, i.e. the wastewater is retained by a valve on the outside.

All these types of toilets do not require much maintenance but they still need a little love especially for the non-return valve at the bottom of the bowl. Make sure all waste goes into the wastewater tank before you close the valve. Also, make sure that no toilet paper or anything else is blocking the valve from closing properly. Unpleasant odors can be transmitted if the valve is not closed properly.

When cleaning the bowl, do not use abrasive, acidic or overly concentrated products. Most toilets are made of plastic and are therefore less resistant than ceramic or stainless steel ones. Moreover, the seal is made of rubber and this material is rather sensitive to strong and abrasive products. Instead, use a mild, non-abrasive soap and toilet paper that you can simply throw in the bowl afterwards. I insist on using toilet paper, not paper towels or even worse, brown paper or wipes. Toilet paper is specially designed so that once in water, it breaks down easily into pieces and is less likely to block your toilet. In short, only organic waste and toilet paper in the toilet bowl or you'll run into problems. Prioritize lower quality toilet paper rather than brands that are touted as extra or ultra strong, in other words, hard to tear. Dealers often sell toilet paper for camping toilets because it breaks down easily, but low-end toilet paper will do the trick and you'll pay less.

How Do You Drain The Storage Tanks?

First of all, the drain hose and check valves are always on the opposite side of the entrance door. This is the standard way that all campgrounds agree on for their field installations and it makes perfect sense. So your pipe and valves should be somewhere on that side.

Your drain hose should have a plug, the purpose of which is to prevent spills in the event of a leak in one or more check valves. Before removing the plug, make sure your valves are closed and then remove the plug by unscrewing it clockwise. Install your hose. Your hose should look like this at best.

The part with the three hooks should grip your drain hose in the same place your plug used to grip it but now in a clockwise direction. At campgrounds or dump stations you have a mostly white 10 cm (4") hose that you can put the other end of your hose on.

The ideal way to make your life easier is to have the 90o elbow that will clamp or screw onto the drain hose coming out of the ground. The installation will be much stronger and will hold up better when you open the valves to drain your tanks.

When draining, the black water tank should be emptied first. If you are at a campground, it is best to wait until the black water tank is at least three-quarters full. When you open the black water valve, there will be more washout and emptying will be easier, more efficient and much less likely to clog. To check or make sure the black water tank is empty, some RVs have a nozzle system inside the black water tank. This allows you to clean your tank when it is empty. If this is the case, you should have a "black water" plug like this one.

In this case, just plug in your garden hose and let it run for a minute or two. Make sure that the valve on the black water tank is open, otherwise if your tank fills up completely with water and pressure builds up, you could damage your tank. Usually this tank has a vent in the roof so if it fills up, the water could come right out the vent. Same thing when you want to hook up to city water, don't confuse the two outlets. I am talking about a real life experience. I made a mistake when I wanted to connect to the city water, I confused it with the black water nozzle. As a result, the pressure in the tank rose and when I tried to flush the toilet, a geyser came out. We learn from our mistakes.

If you don't have this option on your RV, there are tools that you can adapt in series to your drain or water hose that you can pass through the hole of the toilet bowl if your toilet obviously opens directly onto the black water tank.

There are electric valves on the market, or perhaps your RV is equipped with one, that can be activated from inside the RV. Once your hose is connected, you can open your valve from the inside without getting your hands dirty. Don't inadvertently snag the button though.

Now that your black water tank is empty, close the valve and empty your gray water. The gray water is usually cleaner, will clean your hose and will be more pleasant to disconnect and clean.

As I discussed in the electrical module for cleaning level campers, it is recommended to clean your black and grey water tanks. I'll repeat here how to do it if you decided to skip this part.

Use a degreasing cleaner with hot water and put 2 good boilers in each of the tanks and leave with your RV. During the trip, the movement stirs it all up and when you arrive at your destination, you change the oil and often the indicators are back to normal. Do this 2 or 3 times during the season. It eliminates, at the same time, the odors and prevents eventual blocking problems. Ideally, it should be done at temperatures above 24°C (76°F). Grease is more soluble above this temperature.

If you have a leak, it is possible to repair your tanks. Most storage tanks are made of ABS plastic. This is a common plumbing plastic, so you should have no trouble finding what you need to repair it. On the other hand, if your hole is too big, it won't be possible to make it but a small hole between a joint or made by a stone won't be a problem. Note that you can find repair kits at your dealer that can work on any type of tank. Otherwise, here is a method for ABS tanks.

• Completely drain the tank and dry out the entire area around the crack or hole. If the crack is inaccessible, you will unfortunately have to remove the tank.

• If it is a crack, drill a hole about 1/8" (0.3 cm) at each end of the crack. This maneuver will prevent the crack from continuing to grow after the tank is repaired.

• Sand the area around the crack or hole as necessary to allow the adhesive to adhere properly.

• Cut a piece of fiberglass wider and longer than the crack by at least 1 inch (2.5 cm).

• From this step on, use disposable gloves and soak your piece of fiberglass with cyanoacrylate glue. This is a glue similar to super glue but in a less liquid gel and takes a little longer to dry which will allow you to handle it before it dries.

• Place the soaked fiberglass piece with your fingers on the damaged surface.

• Apply a hardener to the fiberglass surface to instantly fix it. This step is optional, but if you're worried about your part coming off before it has time to dry this can be a good option.

Some RV's however have polyethylene tanks. The same material as your fresh water tank. In this case, use the same method as described in the fresh water system section.

The piping on most RVs is ABS. The same material most commonly used in homes. Repairs and leaks are fairly simple to fix. A hacksaw and ABS glue is usually all you need to make repairs. If your sink trap, sink drain or shower drain is clogged, the best method of unclogging I know of is to pour a spoon or two of baking soda and a cup of white vinegar down the drain. This makes a chemical reaction and creates a foam that cleans the pipes. Leave it in for at least fifteen minutes and rinse with boiling water. If it's still clogged, try again, but don't increase the recipe as this could be dangerous.

Some siphons under the sinks have clogs. If this is your case, simply remove it and clean it. When you remove it, put a container under the opening to catch the water and the contents of the trap.

For your information, the black water tank has a vent pipe that usually exits on the roof of your RV. The purpose of this pipe is to evacuate odors, to help when emptying the tank, but especially to evacuate gases such as methane which can be dangerous. There should be a cap that allows air to pass over this hose, check this from time to time. The purpose is to prevent the hose from clogging with debris.

THE HOT WATER TANK

There are two types of tanks found in RVs. The most common type is the insulated tank with a propane burner that heats the tank from below. The burner of this type is located at the bottom and sends its flame under the tank in a pipe that goes through the tank and comes out on its way up.

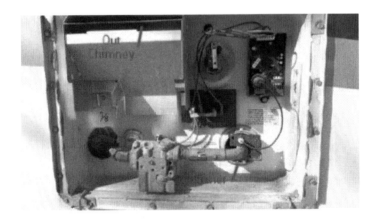

Several sizes are available from 23L to 45L (6 gal to 12 gal). The controls are quite simple, consisting of an electronic gas control valve, a burner, a relief valve and an electronic or manual ignition system.

The other type of tank is not actually a tank. Rather, it is a core of several piping coils heated directly by the burner flame. This model heats water on demand and therefore eliminates the tank. Therefore, its supply is somewhat infinite. It instantly heats the water you use without wasting propane. No need for a big, bulky tank that keeps the water hot even when you're not using it and it requires less maintenance than a tank water heater. It also has a burner at the base of the coil, an electronic gas control valve, a flow sensor, an electronic microprocessor and a thermal sensor. The burner is activated when it detects a flow of water through the coil and is turned off when there is no more water flow and/or the temperature is reached. From the outside, it looks more like this.

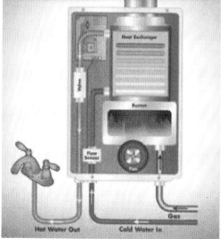

Basically, water heaters run on propane, but some tank models may have a combination of a propane burner and an electric heating element running on 120 volts. Both sources can be used simultaneously to increase the heating rate.

Most tank heaters have an anode on a rod that also serves as a cap. The purpose of the anode rod is to protect the tank from minerals and water hardness. It helps eliminate odors and protects against rust. Replacement of the anode rod is recommended when less than 75% of the material remains. It is very important to replace it because your tank will wear out prematurely and could void your manufacturer's warranty. I recommend replacing it systematically every year, it is an easy and inexpensive task. You will have peace of mind.

General burner maintenance is recommended for all models. As a safety precaution, when servicing the burner, always shut off the propane tanks before beginning your service. Clean off any dust or debris that has accumulated. Make sure the ports are free of dust and deposits. You can clean them with a sharp toothpick to avoid damaging the ports. Check your anode rod, if you have one, and replace the cap or rod. Fill your tank with water. It is very important that the tank is full to start it. In case you forget, there is a thermal protection device that will shut off the gas supply if the tank overheats, full or not. Open your propane tank if you have not already done so, and light your tank depending on the model you have. The model with electronic ignition does this by itself when you press the button inside your caravan. The button usually has a red light. The button should be similar or exactly like this one.

When you turn on your water heater, the light will come on for about a second. This is a sort of test of the light's operation. If after a while the light comes back on and stays on, it means that the burner in your tank did not light. If you have just opened your propane tank, it may take some time for the gas to fill the gas lines properly so that the flame is created. If you want to know if the lines are full, try lighting the burner on the stove. When the flame ignites, the lines will be fairly full. Only the small portion that goes to your tank burner will not be completely full but it will probably be enough to light the tank burner.

Before anything else, make sure your tank is full of water if you don't want to damage it. However, the tanks have a safety thermostat located directly on the tank. If the temperature rises too high, the thermostat will cut off power to the system. It will work whether the tank is full or not, but it is still the kind of device you don't want to see working. This little thermostat is usually visible from the outside panel and is easily changed if it breaks. To test it, when it is cold, the thermostat lets the current through like a switch. If your tank is full of water, it is likely that if the temperature rises too high, the pressure relief valve will open before this device.

For tanks with a pilot light, make sure the propane gas is flowing and light the pilot light with a lighter.

When your water heater burner is lit, take a look at the flame. The flame should be blue in color with perhaps a little orange glow. It should not be completely orange and spitting black smoke. If it is, it means that the gas pressure is not sufficient or that the air/gas mixture is not working properly. If this happens, regardless of the burner check the following things:

• Your burner is properly cleaned and all ports are clear. The ones at the air inlet are also clear. You can also blow compressed air to clean everything properly.

• Check that your other gas appliances are working properly to make sure this is not a widespread problem. If it is and all of your appliances have an orange flame, refer to the gas installations section of the book since the problem is probably upstream at the cylinders.

• You can remove the ports and soak them in alcohol.

• If you feel comfortable, are sure you have cleaned up well and verify that you have enough gas, you can adjust the burner nozzle. A flat head screw or went that is just before the burner orifice.

• If despite all this nothing happens. A part is probably defective. I advise you to check with your dealer. Gas appliances require good knowledge and certification to repair them.

If the gas arrives but the burner does not light, there may be a problem with the electrode of the ignition system or the gas/air mixture may not be correct. You can try lighting your tank with a long-barreled lighter. If the flame lights and the flame is blue, it is probably your electrode that is defective. Check that there is a spark and that the electrode is set correctly to ensure that there is a spark. Note that to have a good spark, the voltage must be between 11 and 14 volts, so if your battery is not well charged, the spark will not occur. Too much voltage is quite rare since the current should go through the converter and in this case, the voltage is filtered. If everything seems fine, then replace the electrode. The electrode is easy to replace, you just have to remove the protector if there is one and pull it off the wire to remove it. An easy part to find at your dealer.

If you have a spark but no flame, you have a gas problem. If your flame previously lit with your lighter but the flame is orange and smoky, it should be cleaned and possibly adjusted as listed above.

Check regularly for soot build-up at the burner flue outlet. If there is, cleaning is probably required and possibly an adjustment.

For tanks with an electric heating element, you will need to turn on the switch that is most likely located near the burner and control of your unit on the outside. Before turning it on, make sure there is water in your tank. An electric heater that is not submerged in water will burn very quickly almost instantly. These elements usually have 1400 watts. Keep in mind that despite the 1400 watts of electric power, the electric heater is still slower than the gas heater. The electric element is coupled with a thermostat placed directly on the tank. The principle of operation is the same as those in our homes. However, it is likely that the terminals of the electric element, the thermostat and the overheat protection switch are hidden behind a protective cover to protect them from the elements. To do the check, you will need to remove these covers. There should be an overheat switch under one of the covers. Unfortunately, this switch may not prevent your element from burning out if it is not submerged in the water in the tank. If the element does not work, check the thermal breaker first and then the electrical panel breaker. Remember that you need a 120V source to power this element. If all the protection devices and switches are still on, check the continuity of the heating element and the thermostat with a multimeter. Also check that the tank is not already very hot and that the thermostat is not already satisfied.

REFRIGERATORS

RV refrigerators work very differently from domestic refrigerators. RV refrigerators work by a chemical and physical process called absorption. Unlike the domestic refrigerator which is a mechanical process. There are actually no moving parts in an absorption refrigerator. This has the advantage of being more resistant to movement, since there are no moving mechanical parts and more versatile than a domestic refrigerator because it uses a heat source to operate. So, in theory, heat sources are easier to set up to operate the refrigerator in all conditions.

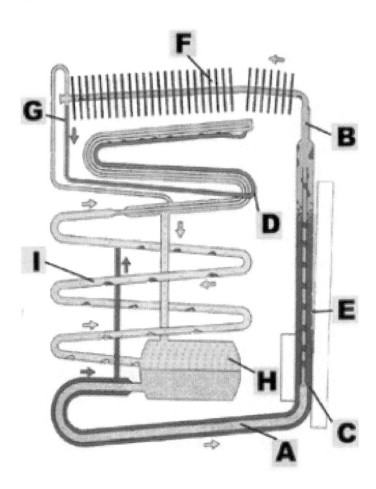

The efficiency of the absorption refrigerator depends mainly on the calorific performance of the boiler, regardless of the energy used, and on the cooling capacity of the ventilation.

As shown in the diagram, the refrigeration circuit represents a kind of obstacle course in which ammonia and hydrogen mix and separate inside a complex circuit composed of pipes whose internal pressure rises to more than 350 psi at certain points.

To begin, a little chemistry is in order. Ammonia is found in the system in three different forms: ammonia in rich solution A. By heating the latter, ammonia gas is extracted B. And the residue of this operation is called lean solution C.

The ammonia, rich solution, pushed by the thermodynamic pressure, enters the boiler E. The boiler, in passing, is part of the kind of chimney that goes to the roof of the RV. The latter is heated by the gas burner or by one of the two heating elements, either 120V or 12V in some cases. Under the effect of heat, part of the solution is transformed into ammonia gas B, the remainder, poor solution, returns in the circuit.

The ammonia passes through the condenser F where it is cooled by the passage of air between the fins, hence the interest in having good ventilation in the rear part of the refrigerator outside the RV. As it cools, it liquefies D and then travels to the evaporator G located inside the refrigerator and freezer.

The chemical reaction of ammonia passing through the evaporator and coming into contact with hydrogen and evaporating causes heat to be absorbed or in other words, cold to be produced.

After leaving the evaporator, the ammonia/hydrogen mixture flows into the absorber tank H and then up into the absorber I. In the latter, the ammonia particles are absorbed by the lean solution which then becomes a rich solution again.

Once the ammonia has been removed, the hydrogen returns to the evaporator. The rich solution returns to the boiler and the cycle starts again.

Note that this diagram represents a typical circuit but there are other principles and other fluids for absorption systems but the principle remains the same. A small amount of sodium chromate is added to reduce corrosion, but it has no effect on cooling.

Absorption refrigerators are convenient, but they have a drawback that they are not designed to run continuously. In fact, with time, the fluid in the circuit will become depleted and the refrigerator will become less efficient. It may end up not freezing your food and running longer. If this happens to you, you should have the fluid changed by a qualified technician.

To operate the refrigerator you have a display panel on your refrigerator. An on/off button. You can have 2 or 3 operating options. The 3 modes are AC, for 120V alternating current, DC for 12v battery and Gas for propane operation. You have a button to set the temperature. You also have an automatic mode that you will use most of the time. The automatic mode prioritizes 120V AC first. If 120V is not available, it will automatically switch to gas mode. If your refrigerator has both AC and DC modes, you will need to select the desired mode.

The following diagram shows typical refrigerator display panels:

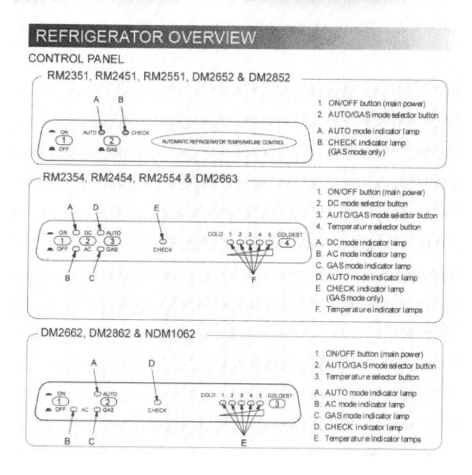

REFRIGERATOR OVERVIEW

CONTROL PANEL

RM2351, RM2451, RM2551, DM2652 & DM2852

1. ON/OFF button (main power)
2. AUTO/GAS mode selector button

A. AUTO mode indicator lamp
B. CHECK indicator lamp (GAS mode only)

RM2354, RM2454, RM2554 & DM2663

1. ON/OFF button (main power)
2. DC mode selector button
3. AUTO/GAS mode selector button
4. Temperature selector button

A. DC mode indicator lamp
B. AC mode indicator lamp
C. GAS mode indicator lamp
D. AUTO mode indicator lamp
E. CHECK indicator lamp (GAS mode only)
F. Temperature indicator lamps

DM2662, DM2862 & NDM1062

1. ON/OFF button (main power)
2. AUTO/GAS mode selector button
3. Temperature selector button

A. AUTO mode indicator lamp
B. AC mode indicator lamp
C. GAS mode indicator lamp
D. CHECK indicator lamp
E. Temperature indicator lamps

The automatic light comes on when your refrigerator is in automatic mode. The refrigerator will default to AC or DC power if you have that option and that is the mode you have selected, otherwise it will be gas mode. When you are in gas mode and the gas flame fails to come on, the check light will come on to let you know that there is a gas problem. It may be that your propane cylinders are empty or shut off. If you have just opened your cylinders and are sure you have propane gas, the lines may not be completely full of gas and the gas may not have made it to the refrigerator yet. When I open my cylinders after a long time of not using them or after running out of gas, I always open my stove

101

rings first to fill the lines with gas until the stove ring lights up. Then we can light the rest of our appliances, it will be much easier. For appliances with the DC option, when the DC light flashes it means that the battery is either too low or too high. The voltage for the proper functioning of the refrigerator in DC mode should be between 10.5 and 15 volts.

Here Are Some Tips For Maintaining And Optimizing The Operation Of Your Refrigerator:

• Cool the refrigerator at least one night before you leave and put your food in it.

• Make sure it is cold before putting food in it.

• For the freezer, put already frozen food in it.

• There should be good air circulation in your refrigerator to have optimal cold. Do not put paper or anything like that on the shelves, it greatly reduces the air circulation and in the process will increase the temperature.

• To reduce frost buildup, put wet liquids and foods in airtight dishes or sealed bags.

• If there is uneven cooling or no cooling at all in gas mode, make sure your RV is level. If your RV is not level, the flame may not be located completely in the center or even next to the boiler. In this case, the refrigerator is less efficient or not working at all and you will not have an indication on your refrigerator.

• Clear the vent outside on the side and the one on the roof well to allow good air circulation.

• Clean the burner regularly and make sure there is no debris or bugs blocking anything.

• If you are cleaning the refrigerator burner, be careful of flimsy holes and small parts. Use compressed air and non-metal tools. A little alcohol to clean the orifices works well.

• When short of a trip, buy food that is already cold whenever possible and put it in the refrigerator quickly.

• As with other gas appliances, the burner flame should be a bright blue. If it is not, it is lacking gas pressure. The flame will need to be cleaned and adjusted. The adjustment valve, as with other gas appliances, is located just upstream of the gas orifice.

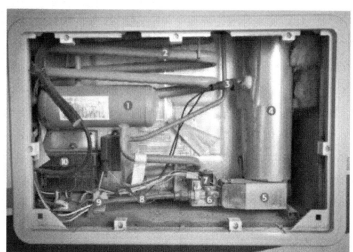

1 Ammonia tank
2 Pipe
3 Electric heater
4 Chimney
5 Burner
6 Manuel gaz control screw
7 Selenoid gaz valve
8 Propane line
9 12V
10 Control box

HEATING SYSTEMS

There is no better system for RVs than the propane forced air system. It works exactly like our home forced air heating systems. The air inside the RV is drawn through a heat exchanger and redistributed through one or more ducts throughout your RV.

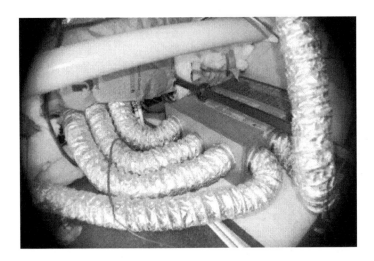

Sometimes with pipes and sometimes not. It all depends on your RV but it's the same thing. The operation is basically the same as a propane water heater.

The thermostat is the main control for the system. Depending on the desired temperature, it opens or closes a contact system much like a switch. In my experience, it is often the thermostat that fails first in heating systems because they are often of poor quality when installed. The original thermostats are rather expensive compared to their quality and efficiency. Can you get a better quality home thermostat for less money? Sometimes yes for the older RV's usually and other times no because the thermostat is in two parts. To find out, look in your RV manual or remove the thermostat. If the thermostat is in two pieces, there will only be two wires in the back. If not, there's a good chance you can put in a much nicer, cheaper and more accurate home thermostat. You'll need a battery-operated central system thermostat.

So what exactly happens when the thermostat calls for heat? The thermostat signals the burner to start. When the heat exchanger temperature is ideal, a timer (another internal thermostat) starts the blower motor and distributes the heat throughout your RV. This same timer also serves as a safety feature. If the heat exchanger temperature becomes too high, it will cut off the power to the burner before any damage occurs, but still allow the blower to run. Another safety feature is the fin switch. This switch verifies that air is flowing through the exchanger. If your blower isn't working, it will cut off power to the burner. Knowing all this now, it gives you a few things to diagnose when your system is not working properly. Here is a typical electrical diagram of a forced-air heating system:

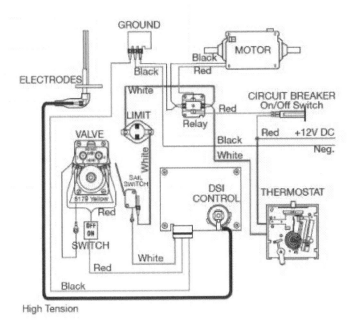

If seen from outside the RV the heating system looks like this:

So no, this is not the way to service it. In fact, the bottom hole is the burner air inlet and the top is the outlet. The chimney in fact. So, to service your system it will be from the inside. How to find it? Look for the air intake grille usually at floor level. Your system will be behind it, often from the top and sometimes from the side. Under a bench, bed or some kind of hatch.

If seen from outside the RV the heating system looks like this:

Here the maintenance is done from the outside. You will notice that in the picture there is only one hole. In fact, not quite. The hole is divided into two parts. The bottom part is the burner air intake and the top part is the chimney. Why the air intake at the bottom and chimney at the top? Well, because the hot air rises and does not end up in the lower air intake, thus avoiding over-heating.

Regular maintenance consists of cleaning the blower and the air intake grille which often does not even have an air filter so it is a real sweeper. Nothing prevents you from adding one if there is space. It will save you from having to do maintenance too often and it will improve the air quality in your RV. However, you will have to check it often to make sure it doesn't get clogged and cause problems. Check the heating system manual to see if adding an air filter will void the warranty. Personally, I think it's better to have one to catch coarse dust and bugs than none at all but it's up to you. If you do, I would suggest not putting the filter directly on the furnace but rather on the wall grill in your RV. In fact, what most manufacturers suggest is not to obstruct the air coming in. A clogged filter is a restriction, but a well-maintained filter is perfect. Between you and me, if over time the fan wheel, the motor and all the components get full of dust, in my opinion, it is much more dangerous.

You can easily find pad style filters in hardware stores that you can size. Avoid using a filter that is too restrictive because it will reduce the airflow and the fin switch may not engage and shut down the burner. Usually, the air intake grills are not very large unfortunately, so this limits the size of the filter a bit. Here is a small example of an installation:

Next is the burner. The burner works in almost every way the same as on the hot water tank. Here I am practically copying and pasting the maintenance of the burner of the hot water tank. To be safe, when servicing the burner, always shut off the propane tanks before starting your service.

When your burner is lit, take a look at the flame. The flame should be blue in color with perhaps a slight orange glow. It should not be completely orange and spitting black smoke. If it is, it means that the gas pressure is not sufficient or that the air/gas mixture is not working properly. If this happens, regardless of the burner check the following things:

• Make sure your burner is cleaned properly and all ports are clear. The air inlet ones too. You can also blow compressed air to clean everything properly.

• Check that your other gas appliances are working properly to make sure this is not a widespread problem. If it is and all your appliances have an orange flame, refer to the module on gas installations since the problem is probably upstream at the cylinders.

• You can remove the ports and soak them in alcohol.

• If you feel comfortable, are sure you have cleaned well and verified that you have enough gas, you can adjust the burner nozzle. A flat head screw or went that is just before the burner orifice.

• If despite all this nothing happens. A part is probably defective. I advise you to check with your dealer. Gas appliances require good knowledge and certification to repair them.

If the gas arrives but the burner does not light, there may be a problem with the electrode of the ignition system or the gas/air mixture may not be correct. You can try to light your burner with a long-barreled lighter. If the flame lights and the flame is blue, it is probably your electrode that is defective. Make sure that there is a spark and that the electrode gap is correct to ensure that there is a spark. Note that to have a good spark, the voltage must be between 11 and 14 volts, so if your battery is not well charged, the spark will not occur. Too much voltage is quite rare since the current should go through the converter and in this case, the voltage is filtered. If everything seems fine then replace the electrode. The electrode is easy to replace, you just have to remove the protector if there is one and pull it off the wire to remove it. An easy part to find at your dealer.

If you have a spark but no flame, you have a gas problem. If your flame previously lit with your lighter but the flame is orange and smoky, you should clean and possibly adjust as listed above.

If the gas is not getting to the burner at all, then check the safety features as mentioned above. Is your blower pushing the air through to turn on the wing switch? Is your wall thermostat working properly? Is the timer relay (thermostat on the exchanger) doing its job?

Check regularly for soot accumulation at the burner flue outlet. If there is, a cleaning is probably required and perhaps an adjustment.

For systems with a pilot light, make sure the propane gas is flowing properly and light the pilot light with a lighter.

In some luxury motorhomes, there are perimeter heating systems that run on hot water. The water circulates by means of a pump in the different room radiators or underfloor heating. The rooms can have their own thermostat. This system produces uniform radiant heat that is more comfortable, more stable and less noisy. The water is heated in a kettle that works in the same way as the domestic hot water tank except that there is a closed circuit with a pump that circulates the water through the different radiators and returns to the kettle to reheat and start the cycle again. Exactly as in a home or commercial hot water system. The maintenance in this case is exactly the same as a hot water tank, so you can refer to the chapter on maintenance.

STOVES AND OVENS

The stove is a key part in RV camping. Despite what one may think, there are not many parts, it is easily dismantled and repaired. Well, for the vast majority of RV stoves. For the rounds and for the oven there are actually 2 types regardless of the model, with pilot light and without pilot light. For the rest, the operation is exactly the same except for some details depending on the model.

As for the stove tops, most of the time they can be removed without any tools, leaving all the mechanics in view. So, for repair and maintenance, there is no problem. Replacing a burner is done in 4 steps:

- Remove the stove cover.

- Remove the burner fixing screw.

- Remove the burner from its orifice.

- Replace and do the reverse procedure.

As simple as that. To replace a burner valve is pretty simple too by following these steps:

- Close the propane cylinders and purge the propane lines by opening another round. Turn on this round to make sure you see the flame go out and make sure there is no more gas.

- Remove the pan cover and burner(s) that are preventing you from reaching the faulty valve.

- Remove the gas inlet line on the manifold.

● Remove the knobs and unscrew the screws securing the manifold so that you can then remove the defective valve by removing the valve mounting bolts.

● Install the new valve without over tightening.

● Replace the manifold as well as the gas inlet line.

● Very important step, turn the propane gas back on and test for gas leaks with soapy water. If there are no bubbles anywhere, you have done a good job.

You may be wondering what tells you that there is a problem with the stove ring, well there are not many parts on a propane ring so the things that could happen are mostly from accidental breakage, misuse or dirt that cannot be removed.

The main cause of a defective valve is that it lets some propane through. You can tell this by the typical rotten egg smell of propane or simply because the flame does not go out completely. Before replacing it, you may want to disassemble it and blow it out with compressed air to remove any small debris that may be present. If there is really nothing to do then replace it.

Obviously, to prolong the life of your stove, it is important to clean it and make sure that all the holes are clear, especially the pilot light if it is the case.

How do we light the pilot light of our stove?

Well, in the following picture, you have a picture of a

Typical stove night light. To get access to it, you will have to lift the cover.

The pilot light is located in the center of the cross under the protector. Follow these steps to light it:

● Check that the gas supply is open and that there is gas.

● Open the small pilot supply valve if so located usually on the manifold following the small pilot supply hose.

● Light the pilot with a long-bill lighter or match.

Virtually all propane ovens have a pilot light. This is for safety reasons to ensure that there is ventilation in the oven and that there is no gas buildup in this enclosed area. There are two main types of pilot lights on propane ovens. I'll show you pictures of both types right now:

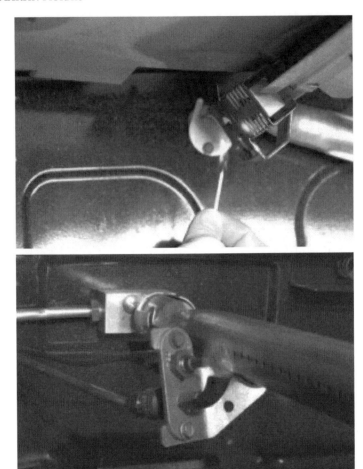

Whether it is one or the other, follow these steps to light it:

● Make sure you actually have gas and that a cylinder is open.

● Turn the oven knob to the pilot position.

● Present a flame on the pilot and press and hold the oven button for about ten seconds once the pilot is lit to make sure it does not go out.

● Then you can turn on your oven.

It may take a little while for the pilot light to come on. If it has been a while since it was lit, the air should come out first and then the propane will come.

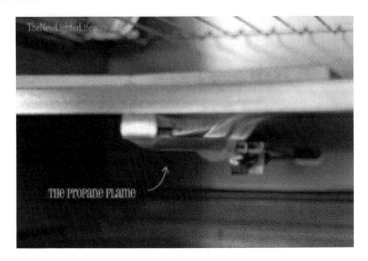

The Propane Flame

All burners in the oven should have a nice blue flame. If the flame is orange or even glowing, the gas/air mixture is not right. Check that all orifices are clear and clean. If everything in the oven looks clean and clear, there may be a faulty thermostat, a faulty oven safety valve, or an orifice that is not letting enough gas through. Check that the stove rings do not have the same problem. If so, it is probably a generalized problem. The cylinder regulator may be defective or dirty. Check to see if the other appliances are working properly. If not, the problem is at the source.

Remember that in all cases, if you replace a part on a gas line yourself, always turn off the propane and check for leaks before reigniting a flame.

ANTENNAS

In this section I will talk about antennas. Nowadays almost all RV's have antennas, even the smallest RV's. There are really many models and I couldn't name them all here. There are really several models and I could not name them all here and anyway I would probably forget some of them because there are so many. One of the most common antennas is the retractable antenna as shown in the following picture:

This antenna has a retracting handle inside which looks like this:

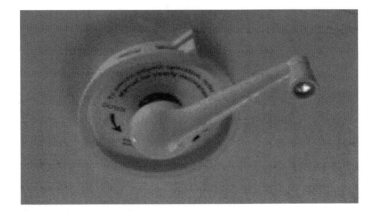

Simply turn the crank to raise or lower the antenna. Once the antenna is mounted, simply pull down the perimeter and rotate the antenna until you have good signal reception. When closing the antenna, make sure to align the two points as shown in the picture so that your antenna will drop down to the right place without catching anything. Note that almost all antennas have a signal amplifier like the one in the following picture. Turn it on to get a better signal.

For this type of antenna there are also signal amplifiers sold separately which fit this antenna. Like in the next picture. Ask your dealer for information.

Retractable antennas like this one or the saucers need a little maintenance every year since there are moving parts and gears. A lubrication of these gears is necessary to avoid bad surprises.

For the rest of the fixed antennas, you still have your signal amplifier but since there are no moving parts, there is no maintenance to do. Furthermore, everything is often encapsulated in a dome.

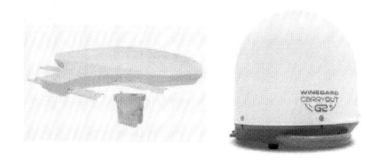

Obviously if you like luxury, there are cable antennas which can be installed on the roof under a dome often like the previous picture but also on the ground. Most RV's have a coaxial socket on the outside to connect a ground antenna to. This antenna is mounted on a stand and it is sufficient to point the antenna towards the satellite. You will have to follow the instructions of the supplier to find the exact spot where it should point. There are even some that find the satellite signal automatically. These are usually the ones under a roof dome.

Awnings

What would an RV be without an awning, this accessory that allows you to enjoy the outdoors while remaining protected from the sun, heat and rain. However, the life span of an awning depends on several factors: maintenance, exposure to the elements, accidents. Your awning will last for years if you take preventive measures for its maintenance and cleaning. Even when your awning is retracted, it will still get damaged because there is always a part exposed to the sun. There used to be devices that, when the awning was retracted, protected the awning. This device greatly extended the life of your awning. Unfortunately, today we don't find them anymore and it was an asset that greatly extended the life of the awning fabric. I would like to say that this is probably why there are no more of them. Anyway, there are always alternatives. There are white protective plastic tubes on the market like the one in the following picture:

When you store your RV, they will protect your awning from the sun. They are usually sold in 48" sections. Unfortunately, this product is not well known and yet you may never have to change your awning with this simple device.

You are probably aware that there are a variety of spray products that protect awnings. In fact, these products will extend the life of the awning fabric by a few years as well. Depending on the quality of the product, the fabric will still be vulnerable to the sun, but this is better than nothing at all because with nothing at all, the first part to degrade on your awning will be the top. The part that is exposed to the sun even when the awning is retracted. If you buy a protective product for your awning, follow the manufacturer's instructions.

When you first open your awning after it has been closed for a long time, inspect it for mildew or stains. If the material is clean enough, clean it with a soft brush, mild soap and water. Stubborn stains and mildew can usually be removed with a household cleaner such as Oxyclean. Clean and rinse both sides of the awning and let it dry completely before closing it. Of course, there are cleaning products available at RV dealerships. It's up to you to decide if it's worth it or not. Most of the time it's exactly the same mix I mentioned above or javelant based but personally I'm not a big fan of javelant for this type of material.

When the awning is clean, inspect it for holes or tears. Very small holes can be filled with a dot of vinyl glue. Larger holes and tears can be repaired with a vinyl repair kit, available at RV repair shops.

A few simple tips, the weight of rain accumulating on your awning can cause costly damage. Lower the awning a little to one side to allow water to drain away. Winds over 30 km/h can damage your awning and your RV. Since you never know when a strong wind might pick up, you can limit the risk by never leaving your awning open when you are not using it and especially when you are not present.

Replacing An Awning

When it comes to replacing an awning, getting a price and placing an order, you will probably be asked for the awning brand, model, color and size. What can help is the presence of a label on the awning tube or on the awning itself, it usually has 2 to 3 sets of numbers and letters that determine the model, size, color and production number. If sometimes you can't find this label, you will have to measure the awning lengthwise.

To measure an awning, it is usually sufficient to measure from the center of the arms to the center. You will get a measurement to the nearest foot with the fabric being about 6 to 8 inches shorter.

Changing an awning is quite simple whether it is electric or not, the procedure is the same except for the wire to connect the electric motor. You will understand that it is almost impossible to do it alone. I say almost because I have already done it alone but I do not advise it. At least two people with a stepladder each. Here are the two most common types of awnings today. This will give you a good idea of how it works:

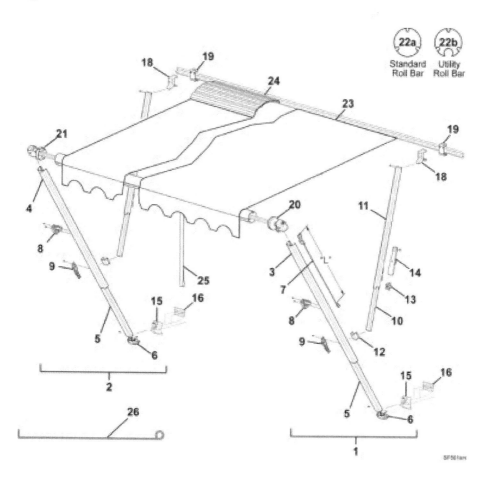

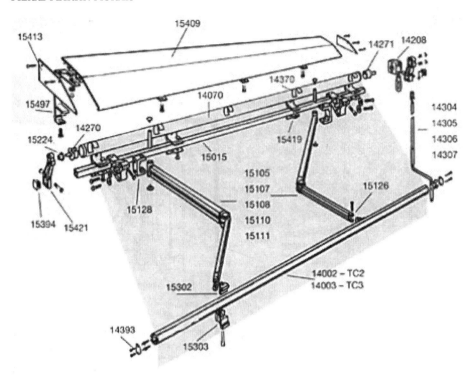

First of all, if you have an electric awning, you will have to disconnect the wire. It is usually located at the top of one of the arms.
You will have to remove the cap at the top of the arm many times
to access the wire. Most of the time, the connector is not directly
accessible so with a pair of long nose pliers, gently pull on the
wire until you have access to the connector and then unplug it.

The top part of the canvas, the one that is attached to the RV
fits into a slide. Simply remove the piece that prevents the canvas from coming out and slide the canvas out. Before doing so,
you will have to detach the roller from its two arms. The roller
actually rests on the two arms at the ends and is held in place
by plugs that normally have only two screws. Remove the two
screws, remove the plugs and then you can take the roller out of
the support arms. Once detached, you can place the roll on the
roof if you can, but if there are several of you, each on his own

stepladder you should be able to slide the fabric out while spanking the roll. Make sure you have enough room to maneuver in the front or back depending on which way you are going to pull the tarp out. The arms, if you change them, are also quite simple to remove. They usually only have two screws at the bottom. Remove them and replace with the new arms. Be sure to use a good sealant with the new screws to seal the holes and prevent infiltration. To put back the new liner, it is the opposite operation of course. Insert the canvas in the slide and slide it to the end, put the roll on the arms and put the plugs back. Simple enough on paper but a bit cumbersome to do. With a few people, you should be able to do it.

If the mechanism inside the roll is defective, I don't suggest you do it yourself. There is a very tight spring inside the roller that could hurt you so leave this job to a qualified technician. If you want to replace only the canvas, it will probably be an impossible mission since you would have to remove the caps at the end of the roll. Many times, the cap is not even removable since it will be glued, sealed or riveted in order to prevent injuries. Therefore, in most cases, the entire roll and fabric will have to be replaced.

COMMISSIONING AND STORAGE OF THE RV.

Winterization

Here are the steps to follow for the winterization of your RV:

First, let's start with the plumbing, the most important aspect in my opinion. Freeze-damaged pipes could cause a lot of problems once spring arrives, and with a little preparation, this predicament is easily avoided. If possible, do RV winterization as early as possible so you don't get caught in the cold winter weather.

● First, empty all of your RV's tanks. The water heater, fresh water, gray water and black water and then flush them out. All of these tanks have caps on the outside of the RV. Locate your tanks and you will find their caps.

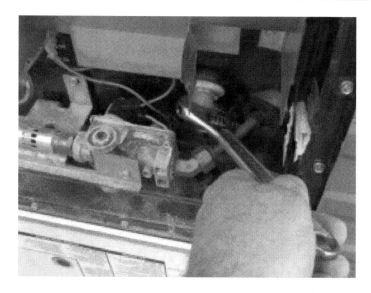

• Newer RVs often have drain hoses that empty your cold and hot water lines usually under the RV. Remove the plugs, then open all faucets and the outside shower. Let the water run, then close the plugs and faucets again.

• Next, introduce antifreeze into your RV's pipes. Use non-toxic RV antifreeze, which is designed for temperatures down to -45ºC. Normally, two gallons should be sufficient.

• Make sure the water heater bypass valve is activated so that the antifreeze does not enter the water heater tank. This valve is located between the inlet and outlet line of the hot water tank so, close the hot water tank inlet and outlet and then open the bypass valve which is located between the hot water tank inlet and outlet.

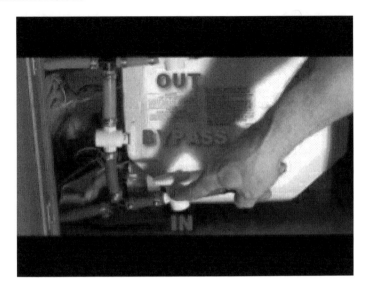

• Using an adapter that you can find at your dealer, the ideal is to blow air out of the fresh water inlet. Open your faucets one at a time to get the water out until only air is coming out. Don't put too much pressure on the water to avoid damaging anything. 10 to 20 psi is enough. Here is a picture of the adapter to help you. This step is optional since you will be using antifreeze anyway, but it's better to prevent it.

• Disconnect the hose from the water pump and insert it into the antifreeze canister to draw the fluid into your RV's pipes. There are three-way valves to make this job easier if you don't already have one. You can get them at a hardware store or at your RV dealer. This valve in the normal position will draw water from the fresh water tank and when winterizing you turn it to the second position so that it will draw antifreeze into your tank with a hose.

● If your pump is hard to reach, you may as well pour the antifreeze directly into the fresh water tank. However, once the winterization is done, I suggest you flush your tank with fresh water. Don't worry even if there is a little water left in your fresh water tank, it won't cause any damage.

● Once the antifreeze is poured, open all the RV faucets, including the outdoor shower and washer, until the antifreeze runs a red color, its true color. This will mean that any water left in the pipes has been flushed out by the antifreeze.

● Pour a good cup of antifreeze down all the drains to flush the water out of the drain elbows. Don't forget the toilet and shower drain to flush out the water and protect them from freezing. Once done, wipe off the antifreeze splashes to avoid staining your plumbing fixtures.

Here is a list of other steps to take when winterizing your RV:

• Make sure you have a full tank of gasoline, to avoid condensation in the case of a motorhome of course and don't forget your generator if it has a separate tank.

• Check all fluids and the freezing point of the engine antifreeze.

• Close, empty and clean the fridge to prevent mold. RV fridges often come with two small spaces to hold the door open all winter. Install them if not, find a way to keep your fridge open to avoid bad odors when spring returns.

• Check the roof and all seals on your RV, to prevent water infiltration. Also lubricate the locks so they don't freeze.

• Close the propane valves, and place the batteries in an area that will not freeze. A battery that has experienced freezing will no longer work.

• To prevent small rodents, remove all paper towels and food and place sheets of fabric softener or mothballs in strategic locations. Rodents can really wreak havoc all over the place. Think even of your sofa, bed and kitchen cushions. Try, if possible, to cover all openings to limit rodent infiltration.

• If you put a tarp on the roof of your RV, make sure it doesn't encourage water and ice. It is important to let your RV breathe.

• Finally, don't store your RV on the lawn. The ground is a very good source of moisture that can create mold, rot and rust prematurely on your RV. If you also have a tarp on your RV it could create moisture inside the tarp.

Putting Your Rv Into Service After Winter

Commissioning is a fun part because it is the beginning of the camping season. There are not many things to check. The main points can be grouped here:

- Recharge, check and reconnect the battery(ies).
- Replace circuit breakers or fuses.
- Turn on fresh water or put some in the tank to properly drain the plumbing of the antifreeze.
- Check for water leaks.
- Replace and open propane tanks and check for odor in your RV. Of course, make sure that all valves and gas appliances are closed.
- Test your gas appliances.
- Check the roof for water infiltration. Check for water stains, walls and ceiling warping.
- Check the condition and pressure of the tires.
- Remove repellent for the smiles.
- Do a visual inspection of your RV outside, especially if you have stored it away from home and could not keep an eye on it. If there is any damage, it is better to see it on site for insurance purposes.

If you find a problem, refer to the part of the book that deals with that problem.

This completes the guide. Maybe there are things I didn't cover in the guide that you would like me to talk about? Write to me at: **travelerguiderv@gmail.com**

Are there things I forgot to discuss or do you disagree with some of the things I said or how I did it? Write me at: **travelerguiderv@ gmail.com**

In any case, I will be happy to answer you and who knows, your question or your subject may be part of another edition.

Thank you very much for choosing my guide and if you are satisfied with it, do not hesitate to recommend it or give it as a gift!

Made in the USA
Columbia, SC
12 April 2022

58859507R00074